ROUND TRIPPER

A Father and Son's Journey

to All 30 MLB Stadiums

and What They Learned Along the Way

C. Shane Hunt, Ph.D.

with

Andrew Hunt

ISBN:1985352389
ISBN-13: 978-1985352384

DEDICATION

To Rodney Loren Pilgrim, our incredible Dad and Papa whose love,
sacrifice, and dedication made every part of our lives better.
We love you forever.

CONTENTS

ACKNOWLEDGMENTS

This book would not be possible without the help, love, and support from many people. Andrew and I want to thank our incredible family—my wife and Andrew's mom Jenifer, and daughter and sister Sarah—for encouraging us throughout the nine years it took to complete our goal.
We also want to thank my mom and dad (Andrew's Grammy and Papa) for being willing to drive with us, sometimes all through the night, to make it possible to see a new stadium. We love you all, and we are forever blessed that you love us.

We want to thank our friends who joined us at different games across the country for being part of this wonderful experience. I want to thank my colleagues at Arkansas State University who encouraged me early on to consider writing a book about this adventure. Special thanks to Dr. Ralph Ruby for the personalized bat he handmade us as a gift commemorating our journey. We want to thank our editor Ann Torbert, who made every page of this book better.

Finally, we want to thank everyone involved with Major League Baseball. We will always remember the incredible players we saw play the game, the kindness showed to us by ballpark employees, and the experiences we shared watching America's pastime throughout North America. Baseball has made our father-son relationship stronger, as we know it has for countless others for more than a century.

1 Chase Field (Arizona)

Play the Long Game

August 8, 2008 – Diamondbacks vs. Atlanta Braves

Early in my life, I fell in love with the game of baseball. I loved the strategy of the game, reading the box scores in my local newspaper, playing fantasy baseball, and watching highlights on *Baseball Tonight*. When ESPN won the rights to televise baseball starting with the 1990 season, I felt lucky that a kid like me, living in a market without a Major League team, could watch live games four nights a week broadcast from different ballparks across the country. I loved the games, and I loved the different look and feel of each stadium and its fan base.

In my first job after I graduated from college, a colleague told me that when he traveled for business, he would always try to see a Major League Baseball game in the city he was in. This guy, in his mid-30s, had already been to 11 Major League ballparks. I was impressed, and so I set a goal for myself: to go to all 30 Major League Baseball stadiums by the time I turned 30 years old. I loved the reaction I got when people would tell me what a great idea that was. But I had not yet been to even five MLB stadiums and had no plan as to how I was going to get to all of the others. Despite the long odds against me, I enjoyed calling it the "30 by 30 Club."

My "30 by 30" plans changed when my wife Jenifer and I found out we were going to have our first child, a boy who was due in January 2002. I had a good job, but like many young married couples, we had no idea about real financial planning or money management. Once our son Andrew was born on January 15, 2002, my thought process and plans changed forever. You learn very quickly that parenting is the ultimate long game. While extended family or friends on social media see the highlights of your child's life (birthdays, sporting events, family vacations), the best part of being a dad is the day-to-day life you have with your children.

As a dad, I have always thought the sport that most resembled fatherhood was baseball. It is difficult and glorious, filled with well thought out strategy and luck, with rules, but with no time limit. Some marketers and critics complain that baseball has lost popularity because young fans do not have the attention span to watch the games or be interested every day for 162-game seasons. I would say this same challenge spills over into how many new dads approach their role. None of us can be the dad we all want to be if we parent on a football schedule and if for only one day a week we are engaged and committed fathers. The link between Andrew's arrival and my love of baseball seemed obvious to me and helped shape my "30 by 30" dream into a new form. The goal I set for myself in my mid-20s evolved into a goal of taking Andrew to every one of the 30 MLB ballparks, which is the story of this book.

Andrew and I went to our first MLB game together in Arizona in August 2008. I had won an award from the American Marketing Association and was going to accept it at the summer conference in San Diego. I had just finished my first year as a marketing professor at Arkansas State University and was excited about the award and the trip. Six-year-old Andrew had already started to love baseball. He and I had been playing the game on the Wii videogame system he had received for his kindergarten graduation. We were sitting in his room watching a baseball game one night and talking about going to his first Major League game. Thinking about my upcoming trip to San Diego, I checked the Padres' schedule. They were not playing in town when my conference was scheduled, but I looked at a map and saw that we could watch a game in Arizona on the way.

The next day I decided we would drive the 2,400 miles from

Jonesboro, Arkansas, to San Diego with a stop in Phoenix to watch the Diamondbacks play the Atlanta Braves. I had bought a new Ford Escape, and since Jenifer wanted to stay home with our one-year-old daughter, my parents agreed to accompany Andrew and me to help with the driving. My parents, Debbie and Loren, were truly incredible parents. This giant road trip reminded me of the time, when I was 11, that our family had driven from Oklahoma City to Disney World all in one night. We had often talked about this, and my parents were excited to have this new adventure with me and their grandson.

The Diamondbacks' stadium, Chase Field, ranks as one of our top-10 favorite stadiums in Major League Baseball. Chase Field opened in 1998 and is the only home the franchise has ever known. It is one of the larger stadiums in Major League baseball, with a regular seating capacity of over 48,000. It has a great kid's area where Andrew got to play and run the bases during the middle innings. While the temperature reached 115 degrees that day in Phoenix, inside the stadium was cool and comfortable. My son, parents, and I were all impressed by the swimming pool in the outfield. The 8,500-gallon pool behind the right-center outfield fence was a way to bring a natural Phoenix association into the ballpark and gave Chase Field a distinctive personality from other ballparks I had seen.

One of my most vivid memories of the game was a guy sitting about five rows away from us who had been drinking and would scream "I Love Stephen Drew" over and over every time the shortstop came up to bat. I guess I could have renamed this first chapter "Don't Get Drunk at Public Events," but Andrew was six years old, and I am not sure if he was fully ready for that lesson just yet. Chipper Jones returned from the disabled list that night with a pair of hits, including a home run estimated at 434 feet, leading the Atlanta Braves to an 11–6 victory over the Diamondbacks. Future MLB Players Association Executive Director Tony Clark drove in a run for the Diamondbacks, and Stephen Drew, possibly inspired from the love he was receiving from our section, homered in a losing effort.

After the game, we waited a few minutes for the postgame fireworks. While waiting, the Diamondbacks showed a great short montage of the opening ceremonies from that night's Beijing Summer Olympics. Sharing the experience of the opening ceremonies with thousands of others, on one of the most impressive video boards we had seen at any event, created a special memory. The fireworks were a great close to the night, and Andrew loved his first Major League Baseball game.

On the way to the hotel and for the rest of the weekend, Andrew kept telling me we should build a Chase Field–size stadium in our backyard. The Disney Channel cartoon *Phineas and Ferb* was popular at the time, and they had done something similar in one of their earliest episodes. Andrew kept asking me when we could go to Home Depot to buy the materials. He also wanted me to confirm the MLB players who would play at our new stadium; he asked if I could call Joe Torre and Manny Ramirez to make sure the Dodgers would be there. The morning after the Diamondbacks' game, as I walked out of the shower with my cell phone, Andrew asked with all seriousness, "What did Manny say?"

I loved going to the game with Andrew and seeing his excitement for baseball. I started to think about my "30 by 30" goal from years earlier and imagined how much more fun it would be if I saw all the stadiums with my little boy. Andrew loved the idea and asked if we were going to see all of them before he started first grade. Since he had only 10 days until school and we had 29 more stadiums, covering thousands of miles, I explained that we would have to "play the long game" and try and see all of them by the time he graduated from high school. I did not talk to Manny or Joe Torre on the trip, nor did we build a Major League Baseball stadium in our backyard. But I did have the feeling in my heart that we had started one of the great adventures of our lives.

Fun Facts

Chase Field (Phoenix, Arizona)

1. The Arizona Diamondbacks, whose home field was the very first stadium on our journey, also was the team we saw the most, with them appearing in five different games.
2. This ballpark has a swimming pool located 415 feet from home plate behind the right-center outfield fence. It's big enough to fit 35 people.
3. Chase Field has an 8,000-ton cooling system, which is the equivalent of air conditioning for 2,500 Arizona houses. This is good, as the temperature gauge in my car read 115 degrees F on the day of this game.

2   Tropicana Field (Tampa Bay)

Don't Live a Lukewarm Life

May 30, 2009 – Rays vs. Minnesota Twins

Our family had planned a short trip to St. Pete Beach the weekend after Andrew finished first grade. We did a bit of research and found that this trip would enable us to make another visit to a MLB ballpark—Tropicana Field, home of the Tampa Bay Rays. We were surprised to learn that the Rays' stadium is in St. Petersburg, over 20 miles from Tampa, and we happily bought tickets to see the Rays play the Minnesota Twins.

Before we left for Florida, I presented Andrew with a gift that a good friend I worked with in the private sector, Don Holbrook, had sent him. I met Don while living and working in Tulsa, Oklahoma. He was originally from Tampa and a die-hard Tampa Bay sports fan. Through our friendship, I think I became one of the few Tampa Bay Ray fans in the city of Tulsa. When I told Don that Andrew had started to really like baseball, Don mailed us a Rays' hat, which still sits on display in Andrew's room to this day. When we went to Tropicana Field that first time in late May 2009, Andrew wore his hat proudly, certain he had found his favorite team. Since that day, Andrew has been a fan and ambassador of all things "Rays"; you will see him wearing Rays' gear in several ballpark pictures throughout this book.

As you drive up to Tropicana Field, the most recognizable exterior feature is the slanted roof. On the Internet, we found out that the roof was designed at an angle to reduce the interior volume of the structure, in order both to reduce cooling costs and to better protect the stadium from hurricane damage. Andrew was amazed by Tropicana Field's cable-supported domed roof (the second largest in the world at the time); it offered six acres of translucent, Teflon-coated fiberglass that looked like something out of a science-fiction movie.

One of the most unique features at Tropicana Field is the 10,000-gallon Rays Touch Tank. The 35-foot-long tank, one of the 10 largest in the nation, welcomes up to 50 fans at a time in a free attraction that allows visitors to touch and feed the 30 rays at their location behind the right-field fence. We took Andrew to this area during the game, and he loved it.

My dad was with us, and he really liked the Ted Williams Museum and Hitters Hall of Fame. The museum is located just past the rotunda in Center Field Street; admission to the museum is free to fans attending the game. We saw an array of different artifacts and pictures ranging from Ted Williams' days in the military through his professional playing career. The museum is dedicated to some of the greatest hitters ever, including Willie Mays, Joe DiMaggio, Roger Maris, and my dad's favorite player, Mickey Mantle.

The game itself was exciting: The Rays were coming off a World Series appearance the season before, and the crowd was optimistic about a return trip to the playoffs. Future All-Star David Price struck out 11 for his first career regular season victory, and Carl Crawford had three hits to help the Rays beat the Minnesota Twins 5–2. The crowd of over 36,000 was much larger than I had expected, and we found out it was in part due to the postgame concert by 3 Doors Down. Today the standard seating capacity for a Rays' game is a little over 31,000, although tarps can be removed to increase that for big rivalries or playoff games (or postgame concerts).

When we got back to the hotel, Andrew was fired up to talk about the game and see the highlights again on television. Every place we went the next week he wore his Rays' hat and let people know he was "all in" for his favorite baseball team. One of the best lessons I have learned as a father is the joy of being all in for things with your kids. Too often our professional lives teach us to have measured responses to positive and negative events, an attitude that then carries over into our personal lives. I never want this to happen to me.

Being a dad and a professor are for me the two best jobs in the world, and they color the entirety of my life for the better. I encourage my children and the college students I teach that one of my greatest wishes for them is that they not live a "lukewarm life." I hope they don't just go through the motions, saying, "I'll get a degree, then maybe a job I don't really like, do that for 40 years, and then die." I want them to find things they truly are passionate about at every age, because I believe that engagement and joy will spill over into other areas of their lives.

I am passionate about being a father—a role that has given me a general sense of enthusiasm and purpose since the day Andrew was born. This trip to Tampa helped Andrew discover one of *his* earliest passions, which has been a constant in his life ever since. With no MLB team within four hours of where Andrew grew up, it is still amazing to me that he chose to be all in for the Tampa Bay Rays, but I am so glad he did. I cannot count the hours I have heard Rays' announcer Dewayne Statts calling a game that Andrew was watching in his room or the number of Rays' shirts and hats we have purchased since that first trip in 2009. My passion to be a good dad and build great memories with my son was the driving force behind the journey we started together. Watching Andrew's passion and support of the Tampa Bay Rays through good years and bad, through Thursday afternoon games in the summer and playoff games in October, has made me very proud. I hope Andrew keeps that passion throughout his life and continues to be all in for his family, for his career, and probably always for the Tampa Bay Rays.

Fun Facts

Tropicana Field (St. Petersburg, Florida)
1. Tropicana Field is the only permanently domed stadium in Major League Baseball.
2. It was the first stadium to have FieldTurf installed.

3. Tropicana Field was the first stadium to host all of the following sports: the NCAA Final Four (basketball), the National Hockey League, college football, and Major League Baseball.

3   Turner Field (Atlanta)

Budget for the Journey

June 8, 2009 – Braves vs. Pittsburgh Pirates

Our first trip to Atlanta was in June 2009 on our way home from a vacation at Disney World. The country was in the midst of the Great Recession, and the Braves had partnered with financial advisor Dave Ramsey to offer $1 tickets to the mid-week game versus Pittsburgh. I was so proud when I found this deal online that I bragged to my wife as if I had completed Ramsey's entire Financial Peace series.

Turner Field was a nice stadium near downtown Atlanta that was originally built in 1996 as Centennial Olympic Stadium, to serve as the centerpiece of that year's Summer Olympics. Converted into a baseball park, it became the new home of the Braves and hosted its first game in 1997. The stadium was nice and clean, but it did feel somewhat bland compared with the other two stadiums we'd visited.

David Ross's bases-loaded infield single in the 15th inning drove in Jeff Francoeur to give the Atlanta Braves a 7–6 win over the Pittsburgh Pirates in a game that lasted almost five hours and gave Braves' Hall of Fame manager Bobby Cox his 2,000th win. This 15-inning game was the longest of any that were part of our journey and included a game-time temperature of 100 degrees. While Jenifer and

Sarah left after a few innings because of the heat, Andrew convinced me that we had to stay for the end of the game. The game featured one of the first MLB starts for Andrew McCutchen, and he was spectacular in the game with four hits, including two triples.

One of the best lessons of our entire 30-ballpark journey is the planning that had to take place for us to finish. While we were sitting in our $1 Dave Ramsey seats, one of the in-game announcements about retirement services led Andrew and me to talk about 401(k)s for the first time. As a seven-year-old, he did not care much about the subject but did appreciate when I described company 401(k) matching funds as "free money." He asked, "So do all employees get this 'free money'?" I said yes, but he was surprised when I told him that a majority of employees I worked with in the private sector did not save enough for retirement to get the full company match, effectively leaving that free money on the table. He said proudly that he would never leave behind money that was offered to him.

Planning is an essential part of being the parent I wanted to be. It was essential to plan if we wanted to see all 30 MLB stadiums together within a decade. It was even more important to plan for Andrew and Sarah's college expenses, dental work, sports and church activities, vacations, and countless other aspects of their childhoods. These things require resources, most commonly money and time, that are finite and must be set aside to reach these goals. My parents sacrificed a great deal so that I could be a first-generation college graduate, and I wanted to provide Andrew and Sarah that same blessing, to be able to start their careers debt-free. I started Andrew's 529 College Savings Account when he was five years old and have made monthly contributions every month since then, plus using a credit card that provides cash back directly into his account for all these years.

Sometime around the 12th inning of that game in Atlanta, I told Andrew that he should be able to retire a millionaire if he wants to. He—and every other young person—has the greatest investment benefit anyone can have: time. The challenge is that the $50 per month people save as 22-year-olds doesn't make them feel wealthy, but it does reduce their ability to dine out or go to the movies. In the short term, the long-term benefit is not always obvious. I had to overcome this challenge personally, and it has shaped so much of my life today. I am not sure this journey would have ever been possible had I not sacrificed some things in the near term in favor of my long-term dreams.

One example: Andrew was 19 months old when I started Ph.D. school at Oklahoma State University, and I was very scared about what I would miss during the years required to complete my Ph.D. Jenifer worked part-time, and I spent many hours planning how we would afford Ph.D. school, how I could fit the schedule required into my working and family life, and what that would mean to our future. Anyone who tells you getting a research-based Ph.D. is fun is either trying not to scare you or is lying to you. For four years, I had to take a reduction in my salary so that I could complete my Ph.D. I refinanced our house at a lower interest rate while also turning our 15-year mortgage into a 30-year mortgage, to lower the monthly payments. We used our cell phones at night to reduce the costs of calling our parents and dined out less to save money. The end result is that I did finish my Ph.D. and have been blessed to have spent more than a decade now as a Professor of Marketing at Arkansas State University. The experience of budgeting for that journey helped me budget for our ballpark journey. I want Andrew to take from our journey that really amazing things are possible but require planning, thought, and determination to get done.

Life is full of budgeting lessons, and this third stop on our ballpark journey was a good example. The next day, Andrew and I discussed the costs of driving, hotel stays, and tickets for each of the 27 ballparks we had left. When that calculation came to some number in the thousands of dollars, Andrew asked how we would be able to do that. Since Andrew was old enough to comprehend addition and subtraction, we turned our baseball trip into a scavenger hunt. Andrew looked at a map on our way home and suggested that to save money we should see the Mets and the Yankees on the same trip to New York (which we did) and do the same with the Giants and the A's on a trip to San Francisco (which we did not). We talked about finding hotel rooms through sites like Hotwire and then, years later, using our IHG Rewards Club points to get free hotel nights (which we did in Kansas City, Cincinnati, and Baltimore). We had started a tradition of buying a baseball at each stadium with the home team's logo on it, and I had Andrew calculate what that cost would be. (There is a picture in this book of all 30 baseballs in a home-plate–shaped glass case. The total for all of the baseballs and frame ended up around $500.) Jenifer mentioned how impressed she was that Andrew was doing all this math and budget planning surrounding baseball. I am better at math as an adult because I studied sports statistics with my parents, and I thought this journey with Andrew provided an opportunity to have a similar positive impact on him relative to budgeting and basic financial literacy.

Finally, I wanted Andrew to know that we were spending the money on the ballpark journey together because of how much we value spending time as a family. Schools can teach kids about how to calculate compound interest and how to do the math required in their finances, but ultimately how Jenifer and I manage our money is a values question. I think Andrew learned a lot along the way that went beyond retractable domes and big scoreboards; I hope one of the legacies of this trip is that Andrew plans and budgets for the great experiences he will have with his children in the years ahead.

Bonus: SunTrust Park

We went back to Atlanta in May 2017 to see the Braves' new SunTrust Park. This stadium, located in the north Atlanta suburbs and part of a larger shopping and entertainment district, is spectacular. The district features a street, called The Battery Atlanta, that leads up to the stadium and is lined with retail, restaurants, and bars. It is a beautiful park with great views and first-class amenities throughout. The seating capacity of SunTrust Park is just over 41,000, down from almost 50,000 at Turner Field.

The reduced capacity and modern design make for a far more intimate ballpark experience—and a very loud one, once the game got started and the Braves scored multiple runs off of Cy Young contender Max Scherzer. The starting pitcher for the game we watched that May afternoon at SunTrust Stadium against the Washington Nationals was Bartolo Colón who at the time was the oldest active player in Major League Baseball. Colón had also started the first game ever in Turner Field in the spring of 1997, making him one of the few players whose career outlasted a new MLB stadium. I told Andrew it reinforces the lesson we talked about previously in Atlanta: You need to budget and plan for the journey, as it can end up being much longer than you think.

Fun Facts

Turner Field / SunTrust Park (Atlanta, Georgia)

1. Turner Field was the only big-league park on our journey that can lay claim to hosting the Olympics' opening and closing ceremonies (1996).
2. In 2013, Turner Field became the first MLB stadium to host a Waffle House concession stand.
3. There are 300 Braves-themed art pieces throughout the new SunTrust Park.

4   Busch Stadium (St. Louis)

The Only Thing We Control Every Day Is How

We Treat People

July 17, 2009 – Cardinals vs. Arizona Diamondbacks

After watching the televised 2009 All-Star game hosted by the Cardinals, Andrew and I decided to make a quick day trip to St. Louis to watch the first game right after the All-Star break. Jenifer and I had been to the old Busch Stadium with friends early in our marriage, where we saw Mark McGwire hit his 550th career home run, but this was our first time at the new ballpark. The new Busch Stadium, with a seating capacity of just under 47,000, was built to face the 630-foot-tall Gateway Arch and the rest of downtown St. Louis's skyline. All the concourses, including the upper level, are open, to allow fans views of the field. The tens of thousands of fans, all wearing Cardinal-red shirts at the game, is one of the most impressive fan displays we saw anywhere on our journey.

Busch Stadium does a great job highlighting the history of the franchise, with one of the most impressive statue collections of any ballpark we visited. We loved seeing the Stan Musial statue when we entered and statues of Cardinal Hall of Famers including Ozzie Smith, Rogers Hornsby, Bob Gibson, and Red Schoendienst outside the team store. Andrew learned a lot about the Cardinals' past by looking at the brick inlays that highlight great moments in the franchise's history. We briefly visited the family pavilion where they had several fun opportunities for kids to hit or pitch, but for the first time since we started going to the ballparks, Andrew was more focused on watching the game.

The weather was perfect (especially welcome, considering it was mid-July), and Chris Carpenter blanked the Diamondbacks over eight innings, allowing seven hits and striking out seven. Cardinals' slugger Albert Pujols, arguably the best player in the game at that time, hit two home runs, including one that landed in Big Mac Land, a special section of seats in the Busch Stadium outfield. Because of the homer, all the fans at the game had won a free Big Mac sandwich which could be redeemed the next day at local St. Louis area McDonald's restaurants.

Andrew clapped with excitement after hearing the good news and asked if we could stay the night in St. Louis so we could cash in on our free sandwich. I suggested we might not want to do that, explaining that a night's hotel stay would cost way more than a Big Mac and offering to just buy him a Big Mac back home in Jonesboro. Andrew disagreed with this plan, arguing with a seven-year-old's logic that the sandwich bought at home would definitely not be the same. I then asked if he would even eat a Big Mac, since I knew he ate his hamburgers plain with just meat and bun (like his dad). "What is on a Big Mac?" Andrew asked me. I told him, as I remembered from the McDonald's commercial, "two all-beef patties, special sauce, lettuce, cheese on a sesame seed bun." With complete sincerity, he said that sounded great and that he would simply ask them to hold the special sauce, lettuce, and cheese, but he said he did like sesame seed buns.

Earlier that night when we had arrived at the game, we were both hungry and went immediately to a concession stand inside the stadium. I still vividly remember (some eight years after the event) the concession workers asking Andrew if it was his first game at Busch Stadium and then taking him over to get some "first Cardinals' game" memorabilia. They took time to ask him what sports he played and let him know they were very happy he was there. Kids have a great sense of who is being genuine and who is not, and Andrew could tell they were legitimately happy he was there. It made him feel great. The ushers, security guards, and many of the fans seated near us shared similar positive moments with us throughout the evening. In all of the stadiums where we have watched baseball (or any other sporting event), I have never seen a place more welcoming to us than St. Louis.

I wanted Andrew to appreciate the experience we had, so we talked about it several times during the game. I think it is important to let Andrew know, often, that how he treats others matters a great deal to me, and it was clear to me the staff at the Cardinals' game had this same culture. As we got back in the car, I wanted to make sure that when we talked to Jenifer about the game, both Andrew and I acknowledged the kindness we had seen. I wanted Andrew to notice, and to know that I noticed, when someone does something nice. To this day, he still comments on how friendly the employees at the Cardinals' game were, and that impression stays with him whether they are winning pennants or not.

I want Andrew to understand that there will be lots of great times in life but also some difficult times. He will work with lots of terrific people, but there will be some colleagues he will probably not enjoy as much as others. He will have good relationships and bad, but every day the one thing *he* can always control is how he treats people. I have seen too many people ruin relationships, miss out on opportunities, or perpetuate bitterness because they allowed a challenge in one aspect of their life to lead them to treat others outside of that situation in a negative way. If I am rude or inconsiderate to a co-worker or waiter, they likely don't think, "I bet he has lots of challenges in his life, and I completely understand why he was mean to me." They likely will think I am kind of a mean person and will not want to spend time being around me, working with me, or talking positively about me.

Andrew is a smart and talented young man, and those qualities will take him far. But I want him to know that the opportunities I have had in life, personally and professionally, and those he will have in his own life, have much more to do with treating people in an honest, genuine, and positive way than any talents or intellectual abilities.

So although we had to pass on the free Big Mac the day after the game, we left St. Louis with a valuable lesson that still resonates for us both. Andrew slept much of the way home, and I remember telling Jenifer in a phone call from the car how thankful I was that our baseball experiences were enabling me to have such conversations with my son and that this journey was strengthening the bond Andrew and I share.

Bonus: Cardinals' Ballpark Village

Andrew and I made a second trip to Busch Stadium in 2015 and were very impressed with the addition of the Ballpark Village. The village includes a three-story, 30,000-square-foot building containing the St. Louis Cardinals' Hall of Fame and Museum and Cardinals Nation Restaurant. Hundreds of seats are located atop the Cardinal Nation section of Ballpark Village, allowing fans to watch the team in action from 500 feet away. There is also the Budweiser Brew House, showcasing Anheuser-Busch's connection to the franchise, featuring a beer garden and 100 different beers.

Fun Facts

Busch Stadium (St. Louis, Missouri)

1. The Cardinals began play in the current Busch Stadium in 2006, becoming the first team in over 80 years to win the World Series in their first season in a new ballpark.
2. The Cardinals' Hall of Fame and Museum collection is the largest team-held collection in baseball. It is second only to the National Baseball Hall of Fame in terms of size, with over 16,000 memorabilia items and hundreds of thousands of archival photographs.
3. The attendance record for any event at Busch Stadium was set by a U2 concert that attracted over 53,000 fans in 2011.

5   U.S. Cellular Field (Chicago)

Make Time to Make Memories

August 7, 2009 – White Sox vs. Cleveland Indians

We took Andrew to Chicago for the first time in the summer of 2009 and experienced many firsts together as a family. It was our first time to go to the top of the Willis Tower, to eat at the ESPN Zone, and to arrive at a ballpark (our fifth) on a train. The Red Line CTA train dropped us within a block of the stadium, which Andrew thought was very cool.

It was an overcast day, and it started to rain that afternoon as we were making our way from the Museum of Science and Industry to the game. While the rain led to a slight delay in the start of the game, it provided one of my favorite visuals from that trip. As we walked in, we saw a man who had gathered some paper towels from the restroom and was attempting to wipe his seat dry. We followed his example and did the same thing to our seats. Andrew loved this activity. He wanted not only to wipe off our seats but also to get more paper towels and wipe off *all* the seats around us. I can still vividly remember Andrew at seven years old wiping off more than a dozen rain-soaked seats at U.S. Cellular Field. You can never predict exactly what your children will enjoy, but this unexpected circumstance made a fun memory for both of us.

U.S. Cellular Field, as it was known then (today it is called Guaranteed Rate Field), opened in 1991, one year before Camden Yards, the first of the "retro" parks, opened in Baltimore. The difference in design and approach is very noticeable. The Chicago stadium, with a seating capacity of just over 40,000, doesn't share the retro style and feel that many of the ballparks built after 1991 have. It is truly a modern ballpark; our outfield seats had a good view, but I remember thinking the section where we were sitting was very steep. The stadium had a lot to offer in terms of quality concessions, family-friendly activities, and promotions. We liked the Fan Deck and the exploding scoreboard, which is the trademark feature. Numerous improvements were made to the stadium over the years including a color scheme featuring lots of dark greens and black steel, which looked nice and clean.

The game itself was well-attended, and Kelly Shoppach hit a two-run homer and added a solo shot, leading the Cleveland Indians to a 6–2 victory over the Chicago White Sox on that Friday night. The Indians won despite grounding into six double plays, tying an American League record at the time. Kerry Wood, playing his first year in the American League, recorded the final three outs of the game for Cleveland.

When we arrived at the park, an attendant asked if it was our first time visiting the stadium. We said yes and were instructed to go to guest services and pick up a commemorative certificate for Andrew. He loved it and planned to put it on display in his room when we got back. As I was paying for food at the concession stand, Andrew looked at his certificate and asked why the White Sox gave out the certificates for free. As a marketing professor I was excited to share the promotional value of that type of certificate and the low relative cost to produce it. He seemed less than impressed with my mini lecture, and asked, "How did they know that people would want the certificates?"

"They knew people would want them because people love having reminders of fun times and great experiences," I responded. "Those certificates trigger happy memories for people when they see them at their house, and they remember the game and who they went with." This led to a great discussion during the pregame about how important it is that we make memories as a family. One thing I learned along this ballpark journey is that there is no better way to show my love for my kids than to give them my time. Time is a tangible expression of how "worth it" Andrew is in my eyes.

One of the great things about watching baseball with your children is the pace of the game and the time you have to talk. Andrew and I have gone together to, and enjoyed, almost every type of sporting event there is, but baseball will always be my favorite. The time talking between pitches, noticing small things together during the game that you can't see on television, and even the longer MLB games provided three hours for us to be together. Making memories is something I treasured at every stop on our journey.

I believe strongly that time is the most valuable thing a person can spend. It is the only thing we can't get back or make up. As a parent, I wanted to be much more than a potty-trainer, chauffeur, tutor, coach, and babysitter. I wanted to be a great dad, teacher, mentor, and life-long friend. While I knew there would be times when I fell short, I wanted to invest my time to make memories with Andrew that he would carry with him long after I am gone. I wanted him to have the memories of what we did and the players we saw but, more importantly, of the time we spent together.

One of Andrew's and my favorite baseball sayings is "Flags fly forever." Every year around the trade deadline, as teams are deciding whether to sacrifice the future in order to try to win the World Series now, we always come back to this simple phrase. Flags fly forever, and championship memories never fade. The memories we have made on this trip are the kind that never fade, the kind that fly forever in your mind and bring you joy as you go through life.

I never imagined that Andrew wiping off wet chairs at a baseball stadium would be something I would remember forever, but I am so glad it is. No matter how our future lives turn out, I am very confident that I will never look back at the time I took to make memories with my children as anything other than the best investment I could possibly make.

Fun Facts

Comiskey Park / U.S. Cellular Field / Guaranteed Rate Field
(Chicago, Illinois)

1. Only one thing was transferred from the old Chicago White Sox Comiskey Park to U.S. Cellular Field: the dirt from the infield.
2. The first home of the Chicago White Sox was located at 39th Street and Princeton, four blocks south of the present Comiskey Park.
3. In 2016, the stadium was renamed Guaranteed Rate Field after a 13-year agreement was signed with the Chicago-based mortgage lender Guaranteed Rate.

6   Miller Park (Milwaukee)

Nobody Talks Funny

April 9, 2010 – Brewers vs. St. Louis

In April 2010, I was presenting a paper at a conference in Milwaukee, and I brought Andrew with me when I saw that the Brewers had a home game during my stay. It was the first week of the baseball season, and the local Milwaukee media was optimistic for a good season ahead.

When we drove up to the stadium, one of the most impressive things about Miller Park was its sheer size. Opened in 2001, the stadium is huge and awe-inspiring in a way very few parks are, and Andrew was impressed from the moment we got there. It was our sixth MLB stadium, and the first time we had witnessed tailgating at the level that we saw in Milwaukee. The atmosphere outside—with tailgaters cooking, drinking, and celebrating in the time leading up to the game—was electric. Miller Park has a seating capacity of 43,000, and it seemed like more than half of those fans were in the parking lot tailgating before the game.

Miller Park's fan-shaped convertible roof (the only one in North

America) guarantees perfect conditions and came in very handy on a cold April night. Weighing 12,000 tons, the seven-panel roof opens and closes almost silently in just 10 minutes. We attended a Milwaukee Bucks' game on this same trip (it was the final week of the NBA season), and the fact that each of the movable panels on the roof at Miller Park were as big as the entire roof of the Bradley Center (home of the Bucks) gave us a great appreciation for the size of the Miller Park facility. In addition, the family-friendly section where our tickets were located was a very nice touch for a father going to a game with an eight-year-old.

Andrew was so impressed with Miller Park that he has always ranked it near the top of all of the stadiums he has been to. He really liked Bernie Brewer, the team mascot, who stands in Bernie's Dugout way up high above the left-field bleachers during games, posting "K" signs, dancing, and taking a trip down his yellow slide whenever a Brewer hits a home run. The game was a low-scoring pitcher's duel throughout most of the night. Nick Stavinoha smacked a pitch from Hall of Famer Trevor Hoffman (the all-time MLB saves leader at that time) into the left-field grandstand, powering the St. Louis Cardinals to a come-from-behind 5–4 victory over the Brewers. Cardinals' manager and future Hall of Famer Tony La Russa praised Stavinoha's big hit in the first blown save of what would turn out to be Hoffman's final season in the big leagues. Although the season had started just a few days earlier, Andrew and I both remarked that the game between these National League Central Division rivals had a playoff-like atmosphere that was more intense than at any of the first five stadiums we had visited. After the game, I forgot where we had entered, which gave us some "quality family bonding time" as we walked completely around the outside of Miller Park in the cold to find our car.

Andrew and I had decided before the Milwaukee trip that to commemorate our ballpark journey, we would purchase a baseball with the home team's logo at every stadium we visited. When we went to the gift shop at Miller Park to purchase a Brewers' baseball, the woman behind the counter asked how we were doing. I said great and made some small talk while she rang up the sale. Once she gave me the receipt, she smiled and said, "You all don't sound like you are from Milwaukee?" I laughed and informed her we were in fact from Jonesboro, Arkansas, and we joked a little about accents. After we left the store, Andrew commented to me that lots of people in Milwaukee "talked funny," which was an eight-year-old's interpretation of different accents.

Andrew's observation led to a great conversation. I wanted Andrew to understand that to the woman at the counter, he and I were the people who "talked funny." Traveling to ballparks across North America, you appreciate the fact that everyone has some type of accent. That accent and how we pronounce words are part of a dialect that also includes the words, phrases, and sentence structures unique to each person's speech. The woman selling us the baseball at Miller Park, for instance, might sound like someone in eastern North or South Dakota, Wisconsin, or northern Iowa—all in a region that predominantly speaks what linguists call upper midwestern English. Andrew and I were both born in Oklahoma and live in Arkansas, and we have a combination southern accent with some "Okie" highlights. Our accents help to illustrate where we are from, and I wanted Andrew to appreciate that. We don't talk funny, nor did the Wisconsin woman talk funny. Rather, we reflect the core of our social and historical identity, interwoven into the fabric of cultural differences.

Knowing the stereotypes some have of southern accents, I asked Andrew if he thought it would be fair to judge someone's intelligence, capability, and character based on how they pronounced a few words. He immediately responded, "No, dad that would be very dumb." I was happy about his quick answer, and a few months after this I was very proud when I heard him remark to one of his friends while watching a movie, "Nobody talks funny, they just live in different places."

As an eight-year-old, Andrew was not completely ready to discuss all of the challenges we face as a society, but baseball and a very nice person behind a cash register in Milwaukee provided us an opportunity to have an important conversation. That conversation at a Brewers' game and all of the people we met on our journey helped me teach Andrew something important: While people may talk different or look different or dress different or have different viewpoints, most all of us share the same passion for the things that really matter, like helping others, loving our children, and enjoying baseball.

Fun Facts

Miller Park (Milwaukee, Wisconsin)

1. The game at Miller Park was the only stadium we ever visited in April.

2. Milwaukee is the only stadium where we saw a sausage race. The Klement's Sausage Race takes place every game at Miller Park at the bottom of the sixth inning. The crowd always stands while the Bratwurst, Polish, Italian, Hot Dog, and Chorizo race on the warning track, around home plate to a finish line near first base. For the record, the Polish sausage has the most wins, followed by the Hot Dog. (Starting in 2018, the Sausage Race will have a new sponsor, Johnsonville Sausage.)

3. The number of baseballs needed to fill up Miller Park is 4,655,926,995.

7   The Ballpark at Arlington (Texas)

Waiting Can Be a Virtue

July 2, 2010 – Rangers vs. Chicago White Sox

My wife was planning a trip to Dallas in July 2010 where we would meet up with Jenifer's parents, sister, and my niece for the weekend. When she asked which weekends I thought would be best, I quickly checked the Rangers' schedule and selected a time when I knew Andrew and I could see our seventh ballpark. We left our hotel in Dallas and headed for The Ballpark at Arlington with my father-in-law. As we left for the stadium, the clouds were ominous, and I was concerned whether the game would be played.

    The Ballpark at Arlington—now known as Globe Life Park in Arlington—is a very attractive stadium with a nice combination of nostalgia and a modern feel to it. One of the first features we noticed were the pavilion roofs over the right-field stands, which reminded me of the columns and roofs that marked many stadiums built in the 1920s and '30s. Texas architecture is featured throughout the stadium, from the outer facade to the Lone Stars in the concourses and on the seat aisles. The proximity of the fans to the game is among the closest we saw at any stadium. The first rows of seats on the first- and third-base sides are just 56 feet 8 inches from home plate. All of the seats in the ballpark are angled toward home plate; the seating bowl cranks in toward the field down both the left- and right-field lines to provide better sightlines. The outfield dimensions are asymmetrical, which is common to many of the ballparks constructed in the 1990s. In Vandergriff Plaza, located just beyond center field, there are statues of Nolan Ryan and Tom Vandergriff, the Arlington mayor who helped bring the Washington Senators to Texas more than three decades earlier.

One feature I had heard about and wanted to see was the office building built into the stadium, enclosing it from left center field to right center field. I was very impressed with how the architectural features of the office building fit perfectly with the stadium. The stadium, opened in 1994, is one of the larger ones in Major League Baseball with a capacity of over 48,000, so it felt like the stadium had sufficient seats. An usher explained to us that the ownership group at the time the ballpark was built (including former President George W. Bush) had an entrepreneurial, business way of looking at the stadium project. The ballpark-facing side of the office building has porches and balconies continuously along every level. Andrew was very young, but remarked to me and the usher that he would someday like to work in an office that is inside a Major League ballpark.

The start of the game was delayed by rain for 2 hours, 25 minutes, but it made for a pleasant July evening that was cooler than normal for north Texas. The Rangers had a very good team that would represent the American League in the next two World Series. Josh Hamilton led off the sixth inning and made the score 3–1 with a 413-foot homer that hit the back wall of the Rangers' bullpen in right center field—below the second deck of seats where his estimated 468-foot shot landed. (That 468-foot drive is listed as the second-longest ever at the Rangers' ballpark.) The Rangers' hard-throwing young closer Neftali Feliz had a rare blown save as the White Sox rallied to win 5–4. The scheduled postgame fireworks show went on as promised and was a great finish to the evening.

Waiting through a rain delay is frustrating for anyone, but especially an eight-year-old like Andrew. One of the challenges of raising a son born in 2002 is that he rarely has to wait for anything. If he needs information, his phone will tell him the answer instantly. If he wants to watch a show, it is ready on demand at whatever time he wants to watch. While we all enjoy the convenience that modern products provide, there are downsides to the device-driven lifestyle. One of those challenges is that with the heavy focus on technology, kids are often overexposed to instant gratification in numerous aspects of their lives. Jenifer and I have tried, and have had success, choosing projects and activities that require time and patience, such as theater, crafts, slower-moving games like Sorry and checkers, and of course, the sport of baseball.

Baseball itself has faced a marketing challenge as some millennials claim they prefer "faster-paced" sports to the slower national pastime. As a father, I think the pace of baseball is part of its charm when raising children. Studies show that learning to wait is a critical skill for children in order to have any measure of success at school. Even though we didn't relish it when we were young (or during the rain delay that night), being able to wait is an important ability for professional and career success. It is something I try both to model for and to promote in Andrew. Baseball provided a great way for him to understand that everything you want does not simply appear. Regardless of one's background and resources, waiting is sometimes essential to ultimately get what we want.

I hope Andrew always remembers that waiting and patience can be a virtue. In a world filled with discourteous drivers, selfish or thoughtless customers, personality conflicts with coworkers, and the constant demands of friends and family, the ability to be patient is probably more valuable than ever. I shared with Andrew at the game that my experience has shown me that a patient person will make better decisions and see more favorable outcomes in life than a very intelligent person who doesn't have the patience to wait for the right time and opportunity. I hope he comes to know that some of the best things in life, including finding the love of his life, landing the dream job, and raising his children, often require lots of waiting.

Fun Facts

The Ballpark at Arlington / Globe Life Park (Arlington, Texas)
1. This game had the longest rain delay of any game we attended.

2. The yellow foul poles down each line were taken from the original Arlington Stadium, which was home to the Rangers until 1994.
3. Globe Life Park sits next door to AT&T Stadium (home to the Dallas Cowboys) and Six Flags over Texas Amusement Park.

8   Progressive Field (Cleveland)

When You Mess Up, Say "I'm Sorry"

August 12, 2010 – Indians vs. Baltimore Orioles

In August 2010, I had to attend a conference in Boston and convinced my parents to make a marathon road trip like the one we had done to San Diego two summers earlier en route to our first game in Arizona. Since the Red Sox were not playing at home when we were to be in Boston, I mapped out the trip to stop in Cleveland which was, as I told my mom, "kind of on the way."

It was my first trip of any kind to Cleveland, and I was impressed with what I saw. Progressive Field was built as part of an urban renewal project that also included Quicken Loans Arena where the NBA Cavaliers play, parking garages, and landscaped plazas. The ballpark, opened in 1994, blends in nicely with downtown Cleveland; its exposed steel design and the vertical light towers mirror the smoke stacks of Cleveland's industrial zone.

Outside Progressive Field, we enjoyed seeing the statues of Hall of Fame pitcher Bob Feller and of Larry Doby, the first African-American player in the American League. Heritage Park behind center field is home to the Indians' Hall of Fame. There are multiple tributes to the early days of Progressive Field (then known as Jacobs

Field) when the Indians were one of the best teams in baseball; from 1995 to 2001, the team sold out 455 straight games. In a feature somewhat similar to Fenway Park's Green Monster, a 19-foot green wall runs across left field. The height of the wall drops dramatically to 8 feet in center field, so a matter of inches to the left or right could be the difference between a double and a home run.

The crowd was sparse that night as the Indians took on the Baltimore Orioles. Progressive Field has a seating capacity of over 35,000, but the ballpark appeared less than half full for this weeknight game. Neither team was in playoff contention, and the August weather was really hot. One of the most surprising memories from this game was when the PA announcer was talking about Baltimore's starting pitcher for that night, veteran right-hander Kevin Millwood. I was watching on the jumbotron as Millwood was warming up in the bullpen, when the Cleveland PA announcer said, "Millwood has had only 2 quality starts in his last 12 trips to the mound." I was shocked they would say that in the stadium while showing Millwood live, where he could hear it. I remember thinking I should distract Andrew in case Millwood gave the camera and the PA announcer an "adult gesture" that an eight-year-old might not need to see. To his credit, Millwood didn't react in that way.

Kevin Millwood *did* have a quality start that Thursday night, but the Indians won the low-scoring game 4–1. Rookie Jeanmar Gómez, the youngest player on the Cleveland roster at that time, pitched like a seasoned veteran, allowing only one run in six innings to get the win. Despite his early success as a starter, Gómez would be shifted to the bullpen within a few years, and we would see him earn a save for the Phillies six years after seeing him for the first time in Cleveland. Michael Brantley had four hits for the Indians, and Chris Perez pitched a scoreless ninth inning, handing new Orioles' manager Buck Showalter only his second loss since taking the Baltimore job a couple of weeks earlier.

When we were in Cleveland that summer, the mood was somber in the downtown sports district because LeBron James had just left Cleveland to sign with the Miami Heat. A person walking up to the stadium next to us showed us where the giant LeBron poster had hung before being removed. One of the big sports stories that month was the letter Cavaliers owner Dan Gilbert had written shortly after LeBron had proclaimed he was taking his talents to South Beach. I told Andrew I thought Gilbert had made a mistake, not because James might come back (because I never thought that would happen), but because of the message that letter would send to potential free agents about how they might be regarded when their careers in Cleveland ended. Andrew's question, "What do you think the Cavs owner *should* do?" gave me an opening to make a bigger point I wanted him to remember: "He should say I'm sorry. He should say it on TV and radio and the Internet."

I explained that we all screw up—most of us on a pretty frequent basis. Once you realize that it is a matter of "when" and not "if" you are going to make mistakes, then you will know that your response can make or break you. I want Andrew to accept the responsibility for what he thought, said, did, or neglected to do. We cannot go back in time or always make things right, but it is important for him to know it's what he does *next* that really matters. Mistakes are part of life and can lead to maturity and wisdom. I told Andrew some of many stupid things I have said over the years. But I also shared how simply saying "I am sorry" and being accountable for my mistakes had helped me be a better father, husband, professor, and friend.

Bonus Trip: Baseball Hall of Fame

The day after we went to the Cleveland game, we spent the afternoon at the Baseball Hall of Fame in Cooperstown, New York. It is almost impossible to describe the beauty and peacefulness of Cooperstown. The Baseball Hall of Fame is a true national treasure and something that can be comfortably seen in one day. Cooperstown has become synonymous with baseball lore, and after visiting we all understood why. Since 1939, the village has been home to the most iconic sports shrine in the game. The red-brick building on Main Street honors and commemorates over 300 of baseball's greats; it fits perfectly into the charming downtown area.

We spent several hours touring the Hall, and each of us had our favorite exhibits. My dad had often talked about listening to the 1956 World Series, and he loved seeing the ball and cap worn by New York Yankees pitcher Don Larsen in the only World Series perfect game in history. I enjoyed seeing George Brett's bat from the "Pine Tar Game" in 1983 which I remembered watching at the time. Andrew was fascinated by the baseballs for all of the no-hitters that were on display.

That night, after we left the Baseball Hall of Fame at closing, we went to a small pizza restaurant across the street. The weather was perfect, and a nice breeze provided a great break from the typical August heat in Arkansas. Sitting there eating pizza with Andrew and my parents, I can remember thinking what a special day it had been. All these years later, this was not only one of my favorite moments of our journey, but one of the 10 favorite days *of my life*. I strongly recommend that anyone who is a baseball fan, or loves someone who is a baseball fan, make the time to see the Hall of Fame and Cooperstown in person.

Fun Facts

Progressive Field (Cleveland, Ohio)

1. The Indians' stadium, formerly called Jacobs Field, set a record at the time with 455 consecutive sellouts between 1995 and 2001.
2. The stadium has a 42-panel, 8.4-kilowatt-hour solar pavilion. It's atop section 541 on the first-base side and produces enough electricity in a year to power an average home.
3. Along the main corridor's third-base side, a trio of brick columns purposely includes an arched look. The design is meant as homage to League Park, home to Cleveland baseball for more than 50 years. That park was demolished in 1951.

9   Kauffman Stadium (Kansas City)

Men's Week

June 21, 2011 – Royals vs. Arizona Diamondbacks

In the summer of 2011, when Andrew was nine years old, we had seen a movie about a father and son taking a road trip together. Andrew loved the movie, and I suggested we could take a road trip, just he and I, that summer. We called it "Men's Week" and decided that the trip should involve baseball and restaurants featured on the television show *Man vs. Food*, which we enjoyed watching. This trip is one of my favorite ideas as a father, and the special one-on-one time has been something we both have cherished.

(By the way, as my daughter Sarah has got older, I have started doing a similar trip with her, in which just she and I go somewhere. Our trips have been to places like the Georgia Aquarium and American Girl doll stores across the country. The same blessing of time spent talking, listening, and growing together that I experienced with Andrew has been one of my favorite parts of our relationship as father and daughter.)

For our first Men's Week, Andrew and I decided to drive to Kansas City where we could see a Royals game and eat at both Oklahoma Joe's Barbecue and Stroud's (two awesome places to eat).

Kauffman Stadium in Kansas City is where I have seen more Major League Baseball games than any other place in my life, and it is certainly one of my personal favorites. Opened in 1973, it is an older stadium that has a timeless quality, with the fountains in the outfield plus lots of new amenities from renovations in recent years. The waterfalls and fountains run for over 300 feet in the outfield on the embankment overlooking right center field. With a seating capacity of over 37,000, Kauffman Stadium offers a wide selection of attractions that Andrew and I enjoyed, including a kids' area known as "the Little K," the Taste of KC which is a right-field sports-bar–themed restaurant, and the Royals' Hall of Fame in left field.

The weather was great for the game against the Diamondbacks. Alex Gordon nearly hit for the cycle, but Wily Mo Peña was the star of the night. Peña hit his first major league home run in nearly three years, and Joe Saunders pitched seven strong innings as the Arizona Diamondbacks beat the Kansas City Royals 7–2 that night. The next day we concluded Men's Week with a trip to the College Basketball Hall of Fame (also in Kansas City), followed by dinner at Stroud's and then the movie *X-Men: First Class* at a theater attached to a casino near the restaurant. We had a great time and definitely found a formula for future adventures.

In the years since, we have taken Men's Week trips to MLB stadiums in Cincinnati and Los Angeles and to WWE events in St. Louis. Next year, Men's Week will involve visiting potential colleges for Andrew out of state. Beyond the fun we have had on these trips, I can definitely say that the one-on-one time with my children has helped keep my unique relationship with each one of them healthy and in tune. Taking Andrew out solo makes him feel special; it says it's worth spending quality time with just him. I have seen this be true when he was 9 years old and when he was 15.

One-on-one time provides an environment in which Andrew or Sarah can share openly without feeling the need to compete with their sibling, and that opportunity is timeless. No matter what the theme, idea, or reason, I don't think you can go wrong spending a little one-on-one time with each of your kids.

Bonus Trip: The 2012 MLB All-Star Game

For several years after Andrew and I started our journey, I wanted us to go to the three-day MLB All-State Game festivities, including the

All-Star Game, the Home Run Derby, the Futures game, and MLB FanFest. When the 2012 MLB All-Star Game was scheduled for Kansas City, the second-closest stadium to our home, I thought this was our chance. In an effort to guarantee my ability to buy two All-Star ticket books for all of the events, in 2012 I became a partial MLB season ticket holder for the only time in my life, when I purchased a 21-game plan for the Kansas City Royals. While I ended up using those season tickets for only one game in September (on our way to an Arkansas State football game versus Nebraska), the 21-game plan allowed me the chance to purchase at face value the All-Star game ticket book for Andrew and me.

The All-Star week experience is something I strongly recommend for any sports fan. Both the Sunday afternoon Futures game featuring top prospects and the celebrity softball games are very laid back and family-friendly. The Futures game we saw included future All-Stars Nolan Arenado, Manny Machado, Jean Segura, and the late José Fernández. The Home Run Derby is exciting but was more of a made-for-TV event at that time. Robinson Canó, who was the captain of the American League Home Run Derby team, chose Prince Fielder, José Bautista, and Mark Trumbo to be his teammates. All of those sluggers were perfectly logical selections, except he did not choose the hometown Royals' Billy Butler. Kansas City fans were not happy about this perceived snub, and they let Canó know loud and clear during the Derby. First, the fans began a "Bil-ly But-ler" chant, then proceeded to boo loudly when Canó came to the plate and to cheer even more loudly each time Canó failed to hit a ball over the wall. The loudest roar of the night came on Canó's closest miss, a ball that banged off the wall just barely short of home-run distance. Canó, after having won the 2011 Derby, failed to hit a single ball over the fence in 2012. Andrew leaned over to me and said he felt kind of bad for Canó and his dad, who was pitching to him during the contest.

When we arrived for the Home Run Derby, after being at FanFest all day, I shared with Andrew a tip so we could remember where we parked. I took out my smartphone and took a picture of the parking section, telling Andrew that even if we forget where we parked, it will be in my phone. Unfortunately, life decided to teach me a lesson: My phone died just as the Derby was ending. Neither Andrew nor I remembered exactly where we had parked, and we got to add about 30 minutes of father-son time wandering around the Kauffman Stadium parking lot. Andrew learned a new tip: The parking-picture tip works only if one's cell phone is sufficiently charged. We decided to celebrate all of the wandering around with a trip to the nearest 24-hour Steak and Shake, which made us both feel better.

The All-Star Game itself was an incredible opportunity for Andrew to see all of his favorite stars in one game. This is a great memory. I estimate Andrew will be able to one day tell his kids about seeing at least 10 future Hall of Famers in just this game alone, including Derek Jeter, Mike Trout, Bryce Harper, and the last All-Star game appearance for Chipper Jones.

The baseball memory I most remember from the game was the complete dominance of the top two National League closers at the time, Craig Kimbrel and Aroldis Chapman. Their appearances late in the game made the hitters look like college players; it was a reminder of how great pitching can control the game, over even the best hitters in the game. We have been to other sports' All-Star events, but none compare to the family fun we experienced that All-Star Week in Kansas City.

Fun Facts

Kauffman Stadium (Kansas City, Missouri)

1. Every seat in the stadium is blue except for a single red seat behind home plate. It was placed there to honor Buck O' Neil, star first baseman of the Kansas City Monarchs in the former Negro League. Buck viewed Royals' games from that very location for years.

2. Andrew and I enjoyed watching the TV show *Man vs. Food* and ate at Stroud's, which had been featured when the show was filmed in Kansas City.

3. Kansas City is the only stadium in which Andrew and I have watched a World Series game in person. We were in attendance for Game 2 of the 2015 World Series, when the Royals defeated the Mets.

10 AT&T Park (San Francisco)

Choose to Be Great

August 5, 2011 – Giants vs. Philadelphia Phillies

As a kid, I remember watching games televised from the old Candlestick Park and noticing the antiquated stadium and many empty seats. When the new stadium for the Giants opened in 2000, I read numerous articles declaring it the greatest stadium upgrade in sports history. While I had been impressed by what I saw on television, watching Barry Bonds set home-run records there, nothing prepares you for the greatness that is AT&T Park. With a seating capacity of over 41,000, the Giants' home is the first privately financed ballpark in Major League Baseball since 1962. Shortly before our visit, AT&T Park was chosen as the 2008 Sports Facility of the Year by *Sports Business Journal* and *Sports Business Daily* as part of the inaugural Sports Business Awards program.

Our seats were in the upper deck, down the third-base line, where the view of San Francisco Bay is breathtaking. The see-through brick wall in right field is a nice touch, and the details throughout the stadium are incredible. As we walked through different parts of the stadium, we could see not only the field and the Bay, but the Bay Bridge and downtown San Francisco behind the third-base line. The quality and selection of the concessions are as good as any sports stadium I have ever visited, and Andrew and I enjoyed eating dinner at the Park. Historical touches are everywhere, from the statues and "Wall of Fame" on the outside, to the thoughtful quotes and murals throughout the concourse. It is difficult for me to imagine a better-designed stadium anywhere in the world.

As a marketing professor and someone who worked in the telecommunications industry, I love the name changes the stadium has gone through and wanted Andrew to know them as well. When the park was first constructed, Pacific Bell paid $53 million to name it Pacific Bell Park, which lasted from 2000 through 2003. SBC Communications Inc. bought Pac-Bell and in 2004 changed the stadium's name to SBC Park. A few years after that, SBC Communications merged with AT&T Corporation (later, AT&T Inc.), which led to the change to the current name in 2006. I worked on deals with all of these companies, and it was fun to reminisce with Andrew about my time in the private sector at Williams Communications and Citynet.

The game we saw featured two of the best teams in baseball at that time, and it was hotly contested. Tempers flared when Phillies' Shane Victorino got hit by a pitch in the lower back, moments after teammate Jimmy Rollins stole second with a six-run lead. Victorino began walking toward the mound, and Eli Whiteside, the Giants' catcher, stepped in front of him. Plácido Polanco then raced in from second base and was tackled by Whiteside. Victorino, Ramirez, and Whiteside all were ejected after benches cleared in the top of the sixth inning of Philadelphia's 9–2 victory over San Francisco.

After the game, Andrew and I walked out of the stadium, prepared to take a taxi back to our hotel. We were unaware of the taxi driver shortage that was problematic in San Francisco at the time and did not yet have any ride-sharing options we were familiar with. We walked around the outside the stadium looking for an available taxi until I said, "Let's just start walking to our hotel, and we'll find a taxi along the way." I felt confident in my plan until Andrew and I had walked over half a mile without seeing any taxis available. When Andrew asked if we were going the right way, I sounded a little like a character from *Finding Nemo* when I said "Just keep walking." I suggested we go down a different street where there might be fewer people in the hope of finding a taxi there. The only thing that changed was that instead of not seeing any available taxis, we did not see any taxis at all. Finally, after walking almost two miles late at night, we arrived back at our hotel.

After that experience, we did not take a taxi to or from a baseball game again until we visited Washington, D.C., in 2015. After the Nationals' game, there was a huge taxi line, and Andrew and I were thrilled to get one quickly. The driver seemed amused by how excited we were to be safely in the back seat of the cab, headed back to the hotel. He said, "I am surprised you are so happy after a Nats' loss." Before I could reply, Andrew said, "That's because you don't remember San Francisco." Andrew still jokes about this episode. Memories of us wandering around stadium parking lots and downtown San Francisco after games are fun times that I am thankful we shared on our journey. (And I'm also thankful they all turned out safely.)

As I was growing up, the storyline I most remember about the San Francisco Giants is that it seemed they were always about to relocate. I had heard stories of the team in the 1970s considering a move to Toronto (before the Blue Jays expansion team) and then in the early 1990s planning a move to St. Petersburg and Tropicana Field. Most often, the desire to relocate was driven by the Giants' frustration with Candlestick Park. With that history in mind, Andrew and I could not believe the incredible stadium we went into that Friday night. Even with all of the new MLB stadiums built over the past two decades, AT&T still stands out for its greatness.

I remember sitting in an interview one time when a senior manager colleague of mine asked the job candidate, "Tell me something you have done in your life that is not mediocre." Although the question was not one I would have asked, I was surprised when the young college graduate did not have an answer. In the years since, I have talked about this story with my college students and my own children. I want Andrew to have an answer to that question. I want him to know that *not* moving forward inherently means you are moving backward. While everyone around you continues to progress, it is essential you do the same or risk losing ground.

In the late 1990s, I read an article ranking all of the MLB baseball stadiums, and Candlestick Park was ranked last. New ballparks were coming online every year, while the Giants continued to struggle to draw fans to a multi-use facility that needed major improvements. Jim Collins' book *Great by Choice* illustrates that even in the most tumultuous business conditions, companies and people can *choose* to be great. The Giants could have built a nice, average, new ballpark that simply provided a pleasant upgrade to Candlestick, especially since they were privately financing the entire project. However, they chose to build something that is truly spectacular—a stadium that makes attending a game in San Francisco feel like an event. The franchise chose to be great, and that decision has forever changed the trajectory of the team.

Like the Giants, most of us have moments in our lives when we face challenges and consider lots of other options. Andrew and I talked a lot about the Giants' stadium history throughout the game in 2011, and I showed him pictures of the stadium changes on my phone. Beyond baseball, I wanted him to know that if you want to be great at any age, you will need to choose to be so.

Fun Facts

AT&T Park (San Francisco, California)

1. In honor of Willie Mays' number 24, the Park's address is 24 Willie Mays Plaza; there are 24 palm trees planted by the front gate; and the right-field wall is 24 feet high.
2. AT&T Park is the only current stadium to have been home to an XFL football team. In 2001, AT&T Park was home to the San Francisco Demons. It was a part of the XFL football league, founded by WWE owner Vince McMahon, which ceased operations after one season.
3. Barry Bonds hit his record breaking 756th home run at AT&T Park on August 7, 2007.

11 Wrigley Field (Chicago)

History Is Cool

September 4, 2011 – Cubs vs. Pittsburgh Pirates

When Arkansas State signed a contract to play the University of Illinois on the opening weekend of college football in September 2010, I immediately checked to see if the Cubs were home that same Labor Day weekend. When I saw they were playing Pittsburgh in a series that weekend, I began to plan for us to drive from Champaign, Illinois, after the football game to Chicago to watch the Cubs' game at Wrigley Field on Sunday.

There are few things as a sports fan that I remember more fondly than walking up to Wrigley Field for the first time. There is a mystique and an excitement that you feel at any age at Wrigley, and you quickly understand why the Cubs have stayed in the same home park for over 100 years. Baseball's second-oldest stadium has a capacity of over 41,000 and offers seating right on top of the action, wonderful nostalgic details, a fun surrounding neighborhood, and the colorful ivy on the outfield wall.

Wrigley Field's ivy-covered fence looks great on television and is even more twisty, tangly, and beautiful in person. Wrigley's distinctive ivy was planted on the walls in 1937 by Bill Veeck (son of a Cubs' executive and eventual owner of the White Sox) and is a true Cubs' treasure. My dad loved sharing stories with Andrew about all of the times he had seen balls get lost in the ivy during games. You gladly give up some modern comforts (even after recent renovations) for the historic value of the ballpark. The food smells incredible throughout the stadium, the sightlines are some of the best in all of Major League Baseball, and the Wrigleyville area outside the stadium feels like a giant block party shared with neighbors.

We never caught a foul ball at any Major League park we visited, but Wrigley Field was the closest we came, with a fan catching one just a few seats away. I thought that coming closest to catching one in Chicago was appropriate, as Wrigley was the first park that allowed fans to keep foul balls. In 1915, owner Charlie Weeghman announced that the team's fans would be allowed to keep balls hit into the stands. The decision was not really intended to please fans; rather, it was an effort to show that Weeghman was a man of means and could afford this luxury. Prior to the Cubs' decision, baseball fans were forced to give the ball back to an usher.

Despite missing out on the foul ball, we all got to participate in the Cubs' ritual of singing "Take Me Out to the Ballgame" with thousands of new friends during the seventh-inning stretch. I think it was the loudest I ever heard my dad sing, and he suggested afterward that Major League Baseball should pass a rule that teams can play that song only during games at Wrigley Field.

The weather that day was perfect, and the game was well played. Randy Wells pitched six strong innings, and Marlon Byrd drove in two runs as the Chicago Cubs beat the Pittsburgh Pirates 6–3 to avoid a three-game sweep. Despite both teams having very bad records on the season, 40,469 fans showed up to take in the game and the Wrigley experience. The Cubs were less than two months away from hiring Theo Epstein and beginning the process that would lead to their first World Series victory in almost a century.

There is no sport in which history is more important and cherished than baseball, and there is no stadium where you feel that more than at Wrigley. On this trip to Wrigley, Andrew heard for the first time about the Curse of the Billy Goat. The superstition dates back to October 6, 1945, when a local bar owner supposedly placed a hex on the club for booting his foul-smelling pet goat out of Wrigley Field. Several people we met at the game wanted to tell stories about Harry Caray, Steve Bartman, and the stadium before it added lights that enabled night games. Andrew was fascinated by all that he heard. It led to a great conversation about how cool history is, how it reminds of us of great times, challenges we overcame, and how we got where we are.

Baseball has been terrific for Andrew and me in developing an appreciation of why history is important, beyond just knowing specific dates for a school exam. The people we talked with at Wrigley felt a personal connection to those stories and told them as partly what happened on the field and partly how it related to their lives at the time. Listening to them share their experiences, and us sharing about our baseball journey to that point, inspired us to talk about writing this book. Andrew was coming up with ideas of things he wanted to write down and share, and to this day he feels a connection to history that I think will benefit him throughout his life.

One of the best parts about the trip to Wrigley was taking my dad there for the first time. My dad was a postman; he went to work very early in the morning and was able to pick me up from school or basketball practice in the afternoon. I can vividly remember him watching the Cubs' games most afternoons when we got home, listening to Harry Caray, and hoping the team would break the curse. I remember us watching the 1989 playoffs against the Giants together. Then in 2003, with one-year-old Andrew sitting on my lap, we again watched the playoffs together, feeling certain that Mark Prior and the Cubs were going to the World Series. Shortly before my dad passed away, while we were talking about different trips we had taken together and reliving so many great memories, he shared that his favorite MLB stadium trip was this one to see the Cubs. He had taken me to my first MLB game at the Houston Astrodome two decades before, and the fact that I got to repay that gift and take him to Wrigley made me very happy.

As I told Andrew a few months ago, when someone you love has a favorite memory, it becomes a favorite memory of yours as well. I knew my dad was smiling in heaven when the Cubs finally broke the curse and won the World Series in 2016.

Fun Facts

Wrigley Field (Chicago, Illinois)

1. The famous ivy backdrop was planted by Bill Veeck in 1937. It was originally 350 bittersweet plants (which would grow faster than ivy) and 200 Boston ivy plants, but the ivy eventually took over.
2. Lights weren't added to Wrigley until 1988. When I was growing up, the Cubs were the only team that did not play night home games.
3. Wrigley Field used to be Weeghman Park. William Wrigley was an investor and kept increasing his shares, then eventually bought out Weeghman in 1918. He was full owner by 1921 and expanded the park in 1922.

12 Great American Ballpark (Cincinnati)

Growing Up Too Fast

August 1, 2012 – Reds vs. San Diego Padres

Our Men's Week 2012 trip was going to include a stop in Louisville to see the Louisville Slugger Museum, followed by a night in Cincinnati to see the Reds play. At the Louisville Slugger Museum, we got to see workers making a bat for Buster Posey in real time as we toured the factory. We loved the area in the museum where you stand in the batter's box while a 95-mph fastball comes toward you. I had never experienced what that felt like, and it made me wonder how anyone could have the bat speed to hit that fast a pitch. It gave us both an appreciation for the incredible strength and eye-hand coordination of Major League hitters. We received a free mini bat as part of the tour and decided to purchase a full-size personalized bat we had made with Andrew's name and the Tampa Bay Rays' logo on it. That bat hangs in his room to this day. The Louisville Slugger Museum greatly exceeded our expectations, and we would recommend it for any baseball fan.

The following night, we had a great pregame meal at Skyline Chili and arrived early for the Reds' game against San Diego. The Great American Ball Park sits downtown near the Ohio River;

despite opening nine years earlier in 2003, it felt very new. The stadium has one of the largest scoreboards in baseball, located above the stands in left field. It is so large it actually blocks the view of nearby U.S. Bank Arena which we had seen as we walked in. The Great American Ballpark has a seating capacity of over 42,000 and strikes a nice balance between recognizing the historical significance of the club while providing a modern game-watching experience.

The original Cincinnati Reds were the first professional baseball team, and the rich history of Reds' baseball can be experienced throughout the ballpark. There's a gap, appropriately named "The Gap," in the stands between home plate and third base, allowing downtown views into the stadium. Our favorite feature was the Riverboat Deck in dead center field—a fake boat that serves as a private-party area and adds to the riverfront atmosphere. The area also has two smokestacks that shoot fireworks in celebration, adding to the riverboat theme. Every seat in the stadium is red, which was unusual but appropriate, and the souvenir stands are named after the Reds' former parks. Giant newspaper displays of historic events, murals, and photo displays of iconic moments are scattered throughout the concourses. As a tribute to Crosley Field, the Reds' home from 1912–1970, a monument was created in front of the main entrance to highlight the park's famous left-field terrace. The grass area of the terrace even has the same slope as the outfield terrace at Crosley Field. Bronze statues of Crosley-era stars Joe Nuxhall (the official address of Great American Ballpark is 100 Joe Nuxhall Way), Ernie Lombardi, Ted Kluszewski, and Frank Robinson are depicted playing in an imaginary ballgame. The rose garden outside the first-base line recognizes the beloved Reds' player and all-time hits leader, Pete Rose.

Before the game, we saw part of the Padres' batting practice and were thrilled when Cameron Maybin hit a batting-practice home run right next to us. Andrew picked it up quickly, and we put it on display in his bedroom when we got home. The game itself was close: Ryan Ludwick led the way for the Reds with a home run and four RBIs. Jonathan Broxton pitched a spotless eighth in his Cincinnati debut, after being acquired in a trade from Kansas City the day before. Aroldis Chapman, whom we had seen dominate American League batters in the All-Star Game the month before, pitched the ninth inning for his 23rd save. I remember a drunk guy screaming his approval for Broxton and nicknaming him "Big Tasty." Several of us in the outfield seats laughed at the nickname for Broxton, which prompted the gentleman to tell us to give him credit for coming up with that nickname once the people on ESPN started using it. While I never heard Scott Van Pelt or Karl Ravech refer to Broxton as "Big Tasty," I hope that guy will appreciate that the nickname got a mention in this book.

The shirt Andrew wore to the Reds' game was one we had bought earlier that summer at the Corvette museum in Bowling Green, Kentucky. The shirt said "Growing Up Too Fast," and I thought how true that saying was. That summer I was busy writing my first marketing textbook; I had spent many hours working on the project and made several trips for meetings with my publisher. It was the first time since we started our journey four years earlier that I felt I was away from Andrew and my family more than I would have liked. Andrew was now 10 years old (we joked about saying goodbye to single-digit ages), and 2012 saw us visit the fewest new stadiums of any year during our journey. I was worried that the little boy whom God blessed me with as a best friend for life was growing up way too fast.

A few weeks after we got home from Cincinnati, a friend who was a new parent asked what my "favorite age" was for my children. After being a dad for almost 16 years now, I can honestly say my favorite age has always been the one my children are at right now. Having a 2-year-old is obviously very different from having a 12-year-old, but each age provides new, different, and unique opportunities to experience with your children. It is impossible to rank-order my feelings when Andrew took his first steps, when he started school, when I coached his church basketball team, when he won a trophy for his science-fair project, or when I taught him to drive. I feel blessed to have had all of these, and thousands of other, experiences with him in the 5,000 plus days we have had together.

I remember reading about a speech Brian Dyson, former President and CEO of Coca-Cola Enterprises, gave at a Georgia Tech University commencement. He asked the audience to imagine life as a game in which you are juggling five balls in the air named work, family, health, friends, and spirit. He suggested that work is a rubber ball which if dropped will simply bounce back. The other four balls, he suggested, were made of glass. If you drop one, it will be forever scuffed, damaged, or even destroyed. I often think of that advice. I never want to drop the family ball, no matter what age my children are.

As I get older, I believe more strongly each day that the most valuable thing in life is time. I can make more money or replace things that are lost, but I cannot get time back. I thought about that idea more on the Cincinnati trip than on any of the others. Regardless of what is happening in other aspects of my life, I want to be intentional to make sure that my family glass ball does not break. Prioritizing my time with this goal in mind led me to write most of my first textbook late at night after the kids had gone to bed or early in the morning before they went to school. The book has been a success, and my favorite personal lesson from that experience was managing my role as an author with my much-more-important role of being a dad. I made a personal pledge to myself that we would not have another year on the journey when we went to only one park, and we never did.

Fun Facts
Great American Ball Park (Cincinnati, Ohio)
1. Cincinnati is a city famous for its chili, and Andrew and I enjoyed a great meal at Skyline Chili before the game.
2. The large analog clock on the scoreboard is designed to look like the famous Longines clock in the Reds' former home, Crosley Field.
3. Cincinnati is a riverfront city, and the sponsored steamboat in the outfield lights up when a Reds' player hits a home run.

13 Coors Field (Colorado)

Remember to Smile

May 30, 2013 – Rockies vs. Houston Astros

We planned to take our first family cruise, a Disney cruise to Alaska, in the summer of 2013. When I saw that the cruise would leave from Vancouver, I pitched to Jenifer the idea that we could make another long cross-country road trip out of it—drive to Canada and see baseball games along the way. After the previous summer when we went to only one new stadium, I was looking for ways to make sure that did not happen again. The two stadiums that were "on the way" to Vancouver were in Denver and Seattle; I waited until the Major League Baseball schedule was released in early September 2012 to book the cruise, so we could see both Coors Field and Safeco Field on the trip.

As a college student in the mid 1990s, I had watched games, in awe, at Coors Field. A high school classmate of mine, Jamey Wright, was drafted by the Colorado Rockies in the first round of the 1993 draft, which is still the highest anyone from my high school has been drafted. Jamey played several seasons for the Rockies, and I would try to watch the highlights of the games that he pitched. The frequency and distance of home runs I watched on *Baseball Tonight*, plus cool features such as heaters in the field to melt the snow, made Coors Field one of my favorite parks—before I had ever visited. It's a true retro park with brick and steel, and it fits right in with the old buildings in downtown Denver.

Coors Field, which opened in 1995, is one of the largest in Major League Baseball, with a seating capacity of over 50,000. Its size was likely a reaction to the massive crowds the team drew in its first two seasons of existence, which the Rockies played at Mile High Stadium. Fans sitting in the row of 865 purple seats located in the upper deck of that stadium watched the game while sitting exactly a mile high (5,280 feet above sea level). The early seasons at Coors Field included record-setting home run totals, due in large part to the elevation at the stadium. To try to adjust for this, the Rockies installed a humidor room, which houses the baseballs that will be used during games. The humidor keeps the leather balls from drying out, so that they will not travel as far at the high altitude. The humidor seems to have been successful at limiting the number of home runs in recent seasons. Andrew did not care much for the science of the humidor, but he was very impressed with the downtown location. I remember him commenting as we walked by a residential area near the stadium that this would be a really "cool place" to live after college.

Our favorite features at Coors Field were the waterfall, water fountains, and surrounding nature area behind center field. The area features seven different kinds of Colorado trees, as well as Navajo ruby sandstone and granite marble boulders. The fountains shoot 40 feet in the air after Rockies home runs and wins, as well as before the game and during the seventh-inning stretch. Wondering how much water that must take, Andrew and I did some research and discovered the fountain and waterfall system recycles 3,200 gallons of water per minute. The natural area of Coors Field wonderfully symbolizes the beauty of the state and the region.

In 2013 the Houston Astros were early in their rebuilding process and one of the worst teams in baseball at the time. While in Denver, they had one of their best series of the year to that point and turned a sloppy start into a rare series sweep. Chris Carter and Matt Dominguez hit consecutive homers during a six-run sixth inning, and Lucas Harrell won for the first time in six starts, as the Astros beat the Rockies 7–5. The game was one of the coldest we attended, even though it was in late May. The sun was out for the first four innings and seemed like a perfect night for baseball. But once the sun went down, my tough son and I were sitting very close together for warmth and wishing we had brought a blanket.

I was very excited as we walked into the game, and 11-year-old Andrew suggested I stop smiling "so goofy." I smiled and told him I was just excited to be at Coors Field with him and on this trip with our family. I definitely smile more than Andrew, or even the teenage version of myself, would probably think is cool, but I wanted Andrew to know how thankful I am for that. I want Andrew to remember to smile as he goes through life and especially when he is talking to people. As a parent (and as a college professor), I try to remember that it is sometimes hard for people to know the difference between anger and concentration, but smiling invites others to engage with you. My mom taught me this lesson, and she is still the best person I have known at doing this each day. Mom smiles at everyone, and a childhood of seeing people's reactions to her made me want to be this way as well. I hope Andrew feels that same way about me when he is a smiling 40-year-old.

Smiling takes some amount of attention and energy. But in smiling at friends, family, and strangers, you acknowledge their humanity, and in doing that, you remind yourself of it and promote warmth and friendship. I challenged Andrew to smile more at people, to find people each day doing service that benefits him, and to smile at them and say thank you for making this day easier.

Andrew smiles a lot now, at least for a teenager, and every time I see him smile it brings me joy on two levels. As Andrew's father, I treasure his smile because I want him to have fun and enjoy the things we do together. As his friend, his smile makes me feel good, and I know the positive influence his smile will have on all kinds of relationships throughout his life.

Fun Facts

Coors Field (Denver, Colorado)
1. Coors Field is made with 1.4 million bricks, each of which has the words "Coors Field" engraved into it. Based on an average brick's weight of 4.5 pounds, the ones used to make Coors Field together weigh 3,150 tons.

2. Under the field are 45 miles of heated cables to help melt snow and green the grass in the early spring.

3. It appears dinosaurs once roamed the area where Coors Field sits. During construction of the stadium, crews found fossils that could be 66 million years old.

14 Safeco Field (Seattle)

"Be Quick, Don't Hurry"

June 10, 2013 – Mariners vs. Houston Astros

From Denver, we went on to Vancouver for our cruise. At the end of the week's cruise, we landed in Vancouver and drove back across the U.S.-Canadian border to Seattle. We had had a great time seeing Alaska and enjoying the shows on the cruise ship, but our kids' favorite thing was the food. Sarah told me she wanted always to live in a place where you can get free chicken tenders delivered to you 24 hours a day. Andrew loved trying all of the different desserts at dinner each night. When we arrived in Seattle, we stopped at an Olive Garden to eat lunch. As we were finishing our meal, Andrew picked up the dessert menu on the table and casually said, "I guess I will go with the chocolate cake." I asked if he was still hungry after that big lunch, and he replied that we was not, but since it was free he thought he would go ahead and get it. I explained that the rules were a little different on the Disney Cruise than at the Olive Garden, where you have to pay for each item. Andrew laughed as he realized he was still living the cruise life; Sarah immediately asked if this "new policy" of paying every time you eat applied only to desserts. When I asked her what she meant, she clarified by asking if we had to pay for chicken tenders each time as well.

Driving to the ballgame, Andrew and I were so impressed by the beauty of Seattle. Safeco Field, which opened in 1999, reflects this magnificent city, with one of the top five stadiums we visited on our ballpark journey. Our seats were in the outfield, but the views were incredible, and the sightlines were the best of any park that we visited. The Children's Hospital Playfield, located on the main concourse behind center field, lets kids play on colorful, baseball-themed equipment. It was easy to access from our seats and definitely one of the best kids' areas of all the MLB stadiums. Our seats in left field were close to The Bullpen Market which featured interactive games and activities for fans, including the Fan Walk personalized bricks, local food vendors, and an open-pit barbecue. This area also has a great view of the ballpark from behind the center-field fence. Safeco Field's HD videoboard is one of the largest in Major League Baseball (57 feet high by 201.5 feet wide) and is easily seen by most of the over 47,000 seats at the stadium.

The crowd was the smallest announced crowd of any game we attended (just over 12,000), but the atmosphere was very upbeat and active with the fans who were there. The weather was nice, so the unique retractable roof at Safeco was open. Most retractable roofs serve to seal a stadium and guarantee an interior temperature; in Seattle, the purpose of the roof is solely to protect the field from rain. That feature is very useful in a city known for rainy days, and the roof's umbrella-styled design let architects create more open areas to see in and out of the ballpark. Maintaining the ability to let fresh air freely waft through the stadium while protecting fans and players from difficult weather conditions makes Safeco Park a place that provides the best of all worlds.

Despite having the worst record in baseball, the Astros were clearly the Hunt family's team that summer, as we saw them in person for the second time in two weeks. Hisashi Iwakuma was someone we had watched on broadcasts of the *MLB Extra Innings* package, and it was fun watching him use all his pitches to dominate the Astros during his splendid start. Iwakuma allowed only an unearned run in seven innings, and the Seattle Mariners beat Houston 3–2. Future Astros superstar José Altuve had two hits in defeat. The Astros' rebuilding efforts would pay off with a trip to the World Series less than five years later.

Talking about our cruise experience during the game, Andrew and I revisited a conversation we had on board the ship. On one of the days at sea, he and I were going to play shuffleboard when we walked past a man on the deck reading a book by legendary UCLA basketball coach John Wooden. As we walked by and saw it, I immediately said, "Be quick, don't hurry." Andrew asked what I was talking about, which led to a great conversation about what Coach Wooden's four-word statement means. It is one of my favorite quotes ever, and one I felt was very important for Andrew to think about as he started his journey as a teenager and into junior high school.

I shared with him that while the quote applies to sports, I believe it also applies to many things he had coming up in life: You need to be quick as you start being a teenager. It is vital to your future, for example, to learn quickly that if you don't study, complete your assignments, and work hard, your grades will show it. I have seen countless college students waste a semester or two, ruin their GPA, and increase their student-loan debt. Without a degree, that debt is like paying for a car that you never get to drive. I also shared the idea that he must be quick in adjusting from the very protective structure of elementary school to the self-accountability of junior high. You are responsible for your actions, and as long as you embrace that responsibility, every new step in the educational journey can be one of the best experiences of your life.

At the same time, though, Coach Wooden's quote captures the need *not* to hurry certain things: Don't try to hurry through junior high, taking the easiest classes you can find. Despite what anyone may have told you, simply passing classes or getting degrees doesn't entitle you to anything. It doesn't guarantee you a job, or a career, or the life you want. If you try to hurry through, learning as little as possible in school and participating in as few things as possible, you will likely not be the type of job candidate any serious company would want.

In sum, I advised, be quick to engage in the incredible experience of school and learning, but don't hurry to the extent that you miss out on the knowledge, skills, relationships, and experiences that will give you the best memories and the highest quality of life as an adult.

As we were leaving Seattle, I commented to Andrew that we

were almost halfway through our ballpark journey. He asked when I thought we would finish, and I said "…probably 2018 or so." As I was driving, I thought in a new way about Coach Wooden's advice: I wanted to make sure that neither of us rushed this journey. I told Andrew I wanted us to finish quickly so we would see all of the parks before he graduated from high school, but I didn't want to hurry, because we were having too much fun along the way.

Fun Facts

Safeco Field (Seattle, Washington)

1. This game had the smallest official attendance of any game we attended on our ballpark journey.
2. The ballpark's one-of-a-kind retractable roof is designed to cover, but not enclose, the ballpark, thus preserving an open-air environment.
3. Safeco Field was host to WrestleMania 19. It is one of only two MLB stadiums where WWE has held its premier event.

15 Angel Stadium of Anaheim (Los Angeles)

Pay It Forward

June 21, 2013 – Angels vs. Pittsburgh Pirates

On our way back from Seattle, we spent a couple of incredible days in Yellowstone National Park, saw lots of bison in person for the first time in our lives, and returned home after being gone for over two weeks. Just three days later, Andrew and I were off again—on a trip to California. Two colleagues and I were serving as faculty chaperones for 12 of our Arkansas State University students who had qualified for the Phi Beta Lambda National Championships in Anaheim (part of the Los Angeles metropolitan area). They asked me as a co-advisor to help drive on the trip and offered Andrew space in the back of the van since we had a bit of extra room.

Andrew loved being around the college students that week, and I wanted to do something nice for the outstanding students who were representing our school that week. After looking at the event schedule and a map, I decided to take everyone to an Angels' game at Angel Stadium, which was just up the street from our hotel. On StubHub, I bought tickets in the upper deck for all of the A-State students and faculty on the trip, and of course for Andrew and me. It was the first Major League Baseball game for several of the students. One of them, Yuchen, was from China and enjoyed her first baseball game ever, while ordering the giant-sized portion of barbecue nachos that came in an Angels' batting helmet. The sight of Yuchen trying to eat nearly her weight in barbecue was funny—an experience she told us she will never forget.

I was impressed with how the Angels had renovated the stadium to a baseball-only park after the Rams' football team left for St. Louis in the 1990s. From the outside, the stadium looked like one of the big, multipurpose stadiums of the 1970s, but inside it was comfortable with a really pretty view in the outfield. The stadium is located down the street from Disneyland, and the Angels were owned by Disney at the time of the ballpark renovation. The talented Walt Disney Imagineering team had its own section of the park in which to let Mickey Mouse–style dreams come to life. As I would expect from any Disney-inspired project, the Outfield Extravaganza rock pile in centerfield contained much more than just a pile of boulders. Shooting water cannons, geysers, and fireworks conjured up memories from movies such as *The Lion King* in the terraced hillside-like design.

The now baseball-only stadium has a seating capacity of over 45,000. Except for the outfield, the main concourses are tucked beneath the stands, which is different from the way parks are designed today. There is an outer concourse near the perimeter fence with plenty of eateries and landscaping. The famous "Big A" electronic scoreboard from the stadium's early days now resides in the parking lot, along the Orange Freeway. One of the highlights inside the stadium is being able to see the actual 2002 World Series trophy which is on public display, encased in glass, on the main concourse in front of the team store directly behind home plate.

In the game we saw, future All-Star Gerrit Cole made his first road start in the Major Leagues and was impressive, getting the win pitching four-hit ball into the seventh inning in his native Orange County. Cole repeatedly hit 100 mph on the stadium radar gun; he retired 11 straight before Albert Pujols' lead-off homer in the seventh, his 488th career homer, off the fake rock pile in left center field. Pujols, who looked dramatically older since we had seen him in St. Louis four years earlier, became the only player we saw homer three times in person during our journey. Pedro Álvarez homered for the Pirates, and a member of my fantasy baseball team that year, Jason Grilli, pitched a scoreless ninth inning to get the save. Andrew and I saw future MVP Mike Trout for the first time in person at a regular season Major League game, after seeing him in one of his final Minor League games in Little Rock before being promoted in 2011.

I had recently read an article that expressed concern about the increasing average age of baseball fans and thought, as a marketer, this game was an opportunity to play a small role in sharing the enjoyment of baseball games with some of my college students. It's important for me as a father to show Andrew that he has the power to have a positive impact on another person and should work to do so as often as possible without the expectation of gaining something in return. Baseball has meant a great deal to me, and I wanted to share that passion with Andrew, and on this trip with some of our college students. In order to increase the number of kind adults and baseball fans in the world, I wanted to provide an example of "paying it forward."

I believe the most effective way to teach Andrew to "pay it forward" is by modeling the behavior. Buying the baseball tickets was not a huge deal in terms of cost, nor did it help any of the students find the perfect job or pay off student-loan debt. But "paying it forward" is not just about grand, expensive gestures. Holding the door open for people, showing respect for those around us, biting one's tongue in times of frustration, paying for a stranger's chicken sandwich, giving your free time for a cause, or buying tickets for a bunch of college kids to see a Major League Baseball game—all are behaviors that teach children that we value others. I hope that I am teaching Andrew those things and how good it makes me feel to help others. "Paying it forward" is something we can practice at any age, in any part of the world, and despite any circumstances that may be surrounding us at that time.

Fun Facts
Angel Stadium of Anaheim (Anaheim, California)
1. Angel Stadium of Anaheim had been the home of the Angels

since their move from Los Angeles following the 1965 season.

2. On Cinco de Mayo in 2015, the Angels broke the record for the most number of people wearing sombreros.

3. Major League Baseball teams have 25-man rosters. Long-time Angels' owner Gene Autry was dubbed the 26th man of the Angels for his unfaltering support for the team, and the Angels have retired number 26 in his honor.

Andrew as a six year old when we started our journey on August 8, 2008. and then our first trip to see the Rays with my parents in 2009.

Our 2011 trip to San Francisco and the incredible AT&T Park.

Our 2012 trip to Cincinnati. Andrew was definitely "Growin Up Fast" as his shirt says.

Our 2015 trip to Nationals Park and our picture with President Calvin Coolidge.

Jenifer and Sarah joined us for our 2016 trip to Yankee Stadium where we saw A-Rod's last game.

Our 2015 trip to the World Series in Kansas City.

Our trip to Oakland on August 8, 2017 completed our journey.

16 Dodger Stadium (Los Angeles)

Find Hobbies That Can Last a Lifetime

June 24, 2013 – Dodgers vs. San Francisco Giants

On that same Phi Beta Lambda trip, my friend Dr. Philip Tew got us tickets to a Monday night game to watch the Los Angeles Dodgers. The drive from our hotel in Anaheim to Chavez Ravine was a traffic nightmare, but it all felt worth it when we arrived at Dodger Stadium. It is a beautiful ballpark, and I felt the history at Dodger Stadium in a way that can be matched only by Wrigley and Fenway.

Stepping into Dodger Stadium today is almost like stepping into it as if it were 1962 when the stadium first opened. The third-oldest continually used park in Major League Baseball, it stands as one of the most unique and picturesque settings in sports, carved into the hillside of Chavez Ravine, overlooking downtown LA to the south and the San Gabriel Mountains to the north. Andrew commented about how big the stadium looked; in fact, Dodger Stadium is the largest current MLB stadium, with a seating capacity of 56,000. Our outfield All-You-Can-Eat seats enabled Andrew and me to eat way too many of the outstanding Dodger Dogs (hot dogs).

The weather was perfect for the game, and as day turned into night, the air was filled with boos for the Giants and chants of "M…V…Puig." Madison Bumgarner was pitching for the Giants, the game was being nationally televised on ESPN's *Monday Night Baseball*, and there was a big-game atmosphere. Our seats were in row 1 in the right-field stands, and we missed catching Buster Posey's home run by less than five feet. The Dodgers' rookie sensation Yasiel Puig hit his seventh home run in 20 major league games. He added a tiebreaking single in the eighth inning against Bumgarner. Future All-Star closer Kenley Jansen pitched a scoreless ninth and struck out three Giants to get the save, in a 3–1 Dodgers' victory. Andrew and I were neither Dodger nor Giant fans, but we found ourselves cheering for Bumgarner, Posey, and Jansen, all of whom were on Andrew's and my fantasy baseball teams.

That was the first summer that Andrew and I had played fantasy baseball together. The Internet and free leagues had made it easier for Andrew and other young fans to play with family and friends. One of the other professors on the trip asked Andrew what his hobbies were, and he answered, "Playing basketball on my school team, playing video games with my friends, and playing fantasy baseball." It is always interesting to hear your children answer questions from people they don't know well, and I was particularly struck by his answer. Later that night in our hotel room, I shared with Andrew how much fun it is for me to think how his hobbies will change as his life changes.

Most of my hobbies have changed since I was in high school except for one that was part of our life that night: playing fantasy baseball. Over half my life ago I started playing fantasy baseball in one of the largest national competitions, which at the time was run by *The Sporting News* magazine. On the first day of my first season of fantasy baseball in April 1994, I was an 18-year-old high school senior, seven weeks shy of graduation. I was so excited to get to play! I have felt that same excitement over the past 20 plus summers, having played in the same competition each year from early April to early October. Following the results of my fantasy team has been part of my day-to-day life six months a year since that Monday in April 1994 when we went to my friend Andy Hicks' house at lunch so I could watch a few innings of my players. (I still remember one of my top players, Kenny Lofton, a renowned base stealer, getting caught stealing a base while we there.)

I remember things about my different fantasy teams across most of the major events of the past two decades of my life. I followed my fantasy team the day I graduated from Westmoore High School and the day I graduated from the University of Oklahoma. I followed my team the day I got married and the day my daughter was born. (Félix Hernández pitched a great game the night Sarah was born.) I followed my team the day I started Ph.D. school and the day I defended my dissertation at Oklahoma State University four years later. I followed my team the day of the bombing of the Alfred P. Murrah Federal Building in Oklahoma City and the day baseball returned after the September 11th attacks. I followed my team the day I left my first grown-up job with Williams and the day I "retired" from the private sector at Citynet to become a college professor. I followed my team the day I moved to Jonesboro (Joe Mauer had a great game that night) and the day I started as a professor at Arkansas State University. I followed my team when I lived in Oklahoma City, Norman, Tulsa, and Jonesboro and while I have traveled to 48 states and several countries. I followed my team with Andrew, and we have talked about players and stats in person at all of the current Major League ballparks from San Francisco to Tampa Bay.

I named my first fantasy baseball team the Shanebo Jaguars because my good friend Scott called me Shanebo. As I started college at Oklahoma, I renamed my team the Shanebo Sooners and kept that name until Arkansas State University changed its mascot in 2008, which led me to switch to my team's current name, the Shanebo Red Wolves. In 2011, Andrew became co-manager of the team, and I started asking his opinion on changes to make to the team. We had a really good year in 2011, and then in 2012, the Shanebo Red Wolves had the best season I have ever had in fantasy baseball: On the last night of the regular season, when Curtis Granderson hit a home run for the Yankees, we realized that the Shanebo Red Wolves could be league champions! The 2012 season finished on a Wednesday night, which meant that Andrew could not stay up until the last game was over. But I will always remember how proud I was that we won this together.

The year we finished our ballpark journey, 2017, was the second-most successful season ever for the Shanebo Red Wolves, and as we watched the classic World Series between the Astros and the Dodgers that fall, we were already scouting out players we wanted to draft in April for our 2018 team. We have loved playing fantasy baseball together, and I hope and believe this is something that will be part of our father-son relationship for as long we live.

Fun Facts

Dodger Stadium (Los Angeles, California)

1. In 2009 the U.S. Postal Service made Dodger Stadium the first-ever sports stadium in the country to have its own ZIP Code (90090). The ZIP Code area is officially designated as Dodgertown, USA.

2. The Dodgers have had a record low number of rainouts for an outdoor baseball stadium. From 1962 to 1976 Dodgers' games were rained out only once. Then from April 1988 until April 1999, not a single game was rained out for 11 years.

3. The largest crowd for any event in Dodger stadium history was when over 63,000 people attended a mass held by Pope John Paul II during his visit to the United States in 1987.

17 PNC Park (Pittsburgh)

Every Moment Counts

August 8, 2013 – Pirates vs. Miami Marlins

In late summer 2013, we drove to a marketing conference in Boston at which I was scheduled to speak. I was disappointed that the Red Sox were not in town any of the days we would be there. Since we were driving and had some schedule flexibility, I plotted different itineraries on Google Maps and settled on one that would enable us to see an afternoon game in Pittsburgh on the way to Boston.

Pittsburgh is a terrific city, with one of the most impressive urban revitalizations I have seen anywhere in the United States. PNC Park, which opened in 2001, reflects the impression we had entering the city and is a beautifully designed stadium. At PNC Park, fans can walk around the entire main concourse of the stadium without losing sight of the field. The trail around the ballpark by the water is one of the prettiest walks you can take at any Major League stadium. The views of downtown Pittsburgh beyond the Allegheny River, and the Roberto Clemente Bridge which ushers fans back and forth, are both even more impressive in person than on television. The Clemente Bridge, renamed in conjunction with the building of PNC Park, closes down to vehicles on Pirates' game days, turning into a pedestrian walkway from downtown, leading visitors past a statue of Clemente. The architecture of the bridge ties in with Pittsburgh's historic Forbes Field, with nostalgia-inducing masonry archways across the entry-level façade, steel trusses, and decorative pillars. The stadium itself feels very intimate; it has only two decks, which makes PNC the first ballpark built with fewer than three decks since Milwaukee's County Stadium in the 1950s. When the park opened, its 38,496-fan capacity was the second smallest in baseball, behind Fenway Park in Boston. The highest seat in the house is only 88 feet from the field

In all of the Major League Baseball games we have attended, I have never seen a more dominant young pitcher than José Fernández, the Marlins' starter that day. The day had begun as overcast and rainy but turned into a hot and humid Pittsburgh afternoon. Fernández had been unhittable early in the game, tired by the fifth inning, and was out of the game after throwing 101 pitches and giving up two runs. I commented to Andrew that Fernández had such great stuff that I think he will win a Cy Young Award before we finish our ballpark journey. Christian Yelich hit his first career home run for the Marlins, off Gerrit Cole, but five shutout innings from the Pirates' bullpen and three hits from Neil Walker helped the Pirates earn a 5–4 win in 10 innings.

Andrew and I had seen José Fernández in the Futures Game in Kansas City the year before. He was someone I thought we would be watching when Andrew was old enough to be married and start his own family. Fernández's death in September 2016 at the age of 24 shook the Marlins' organization and the entire baseball world. As Fernández had become more successful, Andrew and I would both tell friends about the dominance we saw in person that day in Pittsburgh. I am glad we had the opportunity to see Fernández play in his all-too-short career, and as a parent, my heart broke for Fernández's mother and his family.

That offseason, I had the opportunity to become the Dean of the College of Business at Arkansas State University and published my first marketing textbook with McGraw-Hill Education. I was excited about being selected to lead the business school I care so much about and was proud to be one of the youngest business-school deans in the country at that time. However, I knew I was giving away lot of the time flexibility I had cherished all of the years I had served as a professor. These were exciting opportunities for me professionally, but I had a mound of self-doubt if I was doing the best thing for my family. Embracing professional success at the expense of time with the people you love most is an easy mistake that many of us make at some point in our lives. The ballpark journey, which I had originally planned to finish in the summer of 2019 (before Andrew's senior year in high school), became one that I wanted to complete sooner, if possible. Looking back on it, my plan to finish our journey sooner was a way for to me to assure myself that my professional opportunities were not taking away from my most important job, as father.

The shortness of Fernández's life provides lots of potential lessons for my son. When the death happened, the main thing I wanted to Andrew to know is that every moment counts. Not some days, or only weekends, or things involving your friends count, but every moment counts. Not only does your current experience matter, but every experience today, on our journey to see all of the Major League Baseball stadiums, and for the rest of your life is important. Each moment generates its own future consequences of some kind or another.

Not far from the stadium in Pittsburgh is Carnegie Mellon University where Randy Pausch served as Professor of Computer Science, Human-Computer Interaction, and Design. As a professor and a father, I have never seen a more moving event on a college campus than Professor Pausch's "Last Lecture," which he gave in Pittsburgh in September 2007 at the 2008 Carnegie Mellon commencement. In that speech, shortly before his death the next summer, Pausch said something I shared with Andrew when José Fernández died and other times when as a father when I have had to discuss death with my children: "We don't beat the Grim Reaper by living longer," Pausch said, "we beat the Reaper by living well and living fully, for the Reaper will come for all of us. The question is what do we do between the time we are born and the time he shows up. It's too late to do all the things that you're gonna kinda get around to." Every moment counts, and I didn't want to wait until Andrew or I are out of moments to appreciate that.

Fun Facts

PNC Park (Pittsburgh, Pennsylvania)

1. The right-field wall in PNC Park is known as the Clemente Wall. The wall stands 21 feet high in honor of Clemente's No. 21 jersey.

2. The home team's dugout traditionally sits on the first-base side of the field, but not at PNC Park. The Pirates call the third-base dugout their home, which allows their players a great view of Pittsburgh's skyline.

3. PNC Park took just 24 months to build. That is three months faster than any other current park in Major League Baseball at the time of construction.

18 Marlins Park (Miami)

No Substitute for Passion

May 31, 2014 – Marlins vs. Atlanta Braves

Our whole family was on the way to Disney World for a weeklong vacation in May 2014. Since we were taking two cars, I decided that my dad, Andrew, and I would drive ahead and go all the way down to Miami, watch the Marlins, and then drive back to Orlando to meet "the girls."

The drive from Jonesboro to Miami is approximately 18 hours, and we planned to drive straight through. As we got to south Georgia on I-75, both my dad and I were very tired and decided we needed to pick a hotel and sleep for a few hours before finishing the trip. I am a proud IHG Spire Elite loyalty-club member, but there was no IHG property near us; I could not bring myself to pay $130 to spend four hours at a random hotel on the way, so we checked into a $39 a night motel right off the interstate to save money and time. Andrew was asleep in the car when we pulled in, and after we got him into bed, I proceeded to barricade the front door to our room with one of the chairs, as I was not very confident in our surroundings. The next morning, and by next morning I mean four hours after we checked in, Andrew woke up, telling us he'd had the weirdest dream—that I was trying to wedge a motel chair under the handle of the motel room door. I laughed when he said it and pointed to the chair leaning against the door, assuring him it was no dream.

We arrived that afternoon at Marlins Park in the same clothes we had left Jonesboro in about 24 hours earlier. The 37,000-seat stadium, opened in 2012, was new but felt somewhat incomplete in places. The bright colors throughout the stadium, the Clevelander Bar behind the left-field bullpen, and the sculpture behind the center-field fence were all nice touches that gave a local, South Florida flavor to the experience. The park doesn't look like any other ballpark we have been to. For example, to mark the backstop, Miami placed a pair of saltwater fish tanks behind home plate. The two tanks make up a portion of the home-plate wall, shifted with one slightly toward the first-base side and the other toward the third-base side. Each of the 450-gallon tanks was designed for safety for those around them and safety for the fish. An inch-and-a-half-thick shatterproof acrylic glass (using the same material found in bulletproof glass), which can withstand the forces of a hit or thrown baseball, protects patrons. The fish, however, needed additional protection, both from the sun in the shallow tank and from various stadium noises, so local tank experts created a cover for the top to shield them from the harmful elements. Also, the views of Miami through the hurricane-proof glass windows in the outfield are spectacular, and the entire stadium has a very genuine South Florida feel to it.

In the game that Saturday afternoon, Jason Heyward and Freddie Freeman each drove in a pair of runs, to lead the Braves' offense, which pounded out 12 hits. Atlanta went on to beat the Marlins 9–5. Craig Kimbrel got the save by retiring the last Marlin with the bases loaded in the bottom of the ninth inning.

The thing I most remember from this game was Andrew commenting on the lack of emotion in the crowd. It was a small crowd, but there was no buzz between pitches as we had seen at other stadiums. We even talked to a stadium worker who said to us that he couldn't wait for this game to be over so he could go home. Anyone who has ever worked professionally has had multiple days when we felt this exact same way. Andrew commented to me that if the worker dislikes his job that much, he should just get another one.

Andrew was not making an economic argument and knew nothing about the person's education, skills or experience, but he knew he wanted to work at something he liked doing.

One of the things I am most proud of as a parent is that every day since Andrew was five years old, he has known that I love my job being a professor. I love teaching, writing, and helping others, and I am fortunate to have identified a career and position that includes those activities. I shared with him a quote I had heard, that "life without passion can become nothing more than an existence." Since Andrew was born at 5:07 AM on January 15, 2002, I have been passionate about being a good dad. I did not want to simply exist as a father, someone who was there, paid some bills, and counted the days until Andrew could pay his own way. I wanted to be a passionate father, share great experiences with him, explain all of the stupid things I did growing up, and instill in him a confidence that no matter what he ever does, I will love him with all my heart. Along the way, I have made lots of mistakes, got distracted at times, lost my temper, or was less thoughtful than I would have preferred. But I don't believe any of those come to close to altering the fact that Andrew knows I love him and am passionate about his life and our relationship.

Our day in Miami was a great reminder that you can have incredible things (money, cars, a new stadium, and so on), but none of those can substitute if passion is not there. After all, you have to have passion to make the 1,113-mile drive from Jonesboro to Marlins Park in less than 24 hours and ultimately to drive the over 25,000 miles we drove together completing our ballpark journey.

Fun Facts

Marlins Park (Miami, Florida)

1. Marlins Park houses a bobble-head museum. Nearly 700 bobble-heads—of Marlins' players new and old, other current and former MLB athletes, and even mascots and broadcasters—sit inside a glass case. The structure holding the bobble-heads moves constantly at a barely noticeable rate, in order to keep the baseball figurines bobbing away.

2. Marlins Park includes a one-of-a-kind, three-panel moving roof that has become the signature architectural feature of the park. Walter P. Moore designed the roof to survive hurricanes with the roof panels in a slightly open, or "gapped," position.
3. Standing 73 feet tall, the outfield sculpture was commissioned as part of Miami-Dade's Art in Public Places program. The sculpture by well-regarded artist Red Grooms is named "Homer" and cost $2.5 million.

19 Minute Maid Park (Houston)

Live Life with a Sense of Urgency

July 26, 2014 – Astros vs. Miami Marlins

I had been serving as business school dean for a little over a month, and already I really missed the time flexibility in the summer that I had when I was only a professor. Our 2014 Men's Week trip needed to be relatively close geographically due to my busier schedule, so we picked Houston, with plans to take my parents with us and visit NASA while we were there.

Minute Maid Park in Houston was stadium number 19, and it will always have a special place in my heart: It was the last game and stadium that my dad went to before he passed away the following spring from cancer. In a strange twist of fate, Houston was the last baseball game my dad attended with me, as well as the first Major League Baseball game he and I went to, in the summer of 1991. I can remember as a 15-year-old the impression the Astrodome made on me and how much I enjoyed watching the game that night, a contest between Houston and the upstart Atlanta Braves.

Minute Maid Park, in downtown Houston, is very impressive, with a large stadium entrance inside the former Houston Union Station. Opened in 2000, with a capacity just under 41,000, the stadium has a retractable roof that made it very comfortable for a July game in south Texas. The wall of glass in right and center fields made the game feel like outdoor baseball. There are over 50,000 square feet of glass on that west wall of the stadium, and the views of Houston are a great part of the experience. The slope in centerfield (Tal's Hill, which was removed several years later) was fun to witness in person, and the amenities inside the stadium were really nice. Over 2,500 seats, known as the Crawford Boxes, extend out into left field, making the distance for a home run just 315 feet at the left-field foul pole. Behind the left field seats is the Phillips 66 Home Run Alley; it features images of memorable Astros' moments and allows fans to take a picture with an old-fashioned gas pump that counts the number of home runs hit at the ballpark. We loved the 57-foot, 24-ton, full-size replica of a 19th-century Wild West steam locomotive that runs on an 800-foot track located above left field.

The game against Miami was exciting as Giancarlo Stanton hit a three-run double and Jordany Valdespin added a two-run home run to power the Marlins to a 7–3 victory over Houston. Future American League MVP José Altuve had three hits in a losing effort. After the game, Jason Derulo performed a postgame concert which I am pretty sure was my mom's first exposure to the man, who sang "Talk Dirty to Me."

When we moved to Jonesboro, after I finished my Ph.D. and was about to start my job as a marketing professor at Arkansas State University, my semi-retired parents decided to move to Jonesboro as well. Those first seven and a half years, before my dad got sick, were a special time for our family. We went together to baseball stadiums and on cruises and trips to Disney World plus lots of Andrew's and Sarah's school and church events. It was often a logistical, and sometimes a financial, challenge to do some of these things; often there was a temptation to wait and do them sometime in the future. However, my dad's illness was a poignant reminder to Andrew (and to all of the family) that none of us is promised another day and that we should not waste the time with which we have been blessed. I am thankful for every trip and experience our family got to share, and also thankful for the sense of urgency that helped Andrew and me finish the ballpark journey a couple of years earlier than our original 2019 plan.

A sense of urgency comes, first, from the extent to which we perceive a situation or problem as important. There is nothing more important than our family, than the people who love us no matter what, but sometimes we take that love for granted. Sadly, serious illness or death often spurs us to reset our priorities, but I want Andrew not to take for granted the time we have and not to wait for those difficult situations before prioritizing his family. Second, a sense of urgency often depends on whether a specific situation or problem requires deliberate versus swift or urgent action. I hope Andrew feels a sense of urgency to do things he is passionate about in life and to be swift and urgent in telling the people most important in his life that he loves them. I hope he seizes the opportunities that life offers, rather than waiting for some fictional point in the future when everything will be easier.

During one of the last conversations my dad and I had in the spring of 2015, he said that the last seven years with all of us in Jonesboro were the happiest years of his life. I want Andrew to know that time runs out for all of us, but I hope that when my time comes, I can say the same thing my dad said. I loved that the first and last MLB stadium we went to together was in Houston, and I know that my dad has been with us in completing the ballpark journey we started with him.

Fun Facts

Minute Maid Park (Houston, Texas)

1. On October 9, 2005, Minute Maid Park hosted the longest postseason game in Major League Baseball history to date, both in terms of time and number of innings. The Astros defeated the Atlanta Braves 7–6 in a game lasting 18 innings, which took 5 hours and 50 minutes to play.

2. Tal's Hill, which was removed in 2016, was a 90-foot-wide, 30-degree incline in the outfield at Minute Maid Park It was named after former Astros' President Tal Smith, who proposed its inclusion as a way to make the ballpark special. Running up the hill while tracking a fly ball, and avoiding the flagpole at the top of the hill, challenged many outfielders over the years.

3. Minute Maid Park is the only current MLB stadium that has

been home to an American and National League team in the past 50 years. The Astros were a National League team when the stadium opened and moved to the American League in 2013.

20 Oriole Park at Camden Yards (Baltimore)

Take Time to Reflect

August 1, 2015 – Orioles vs. Detroit Tigers

This game was part of another family trip scheduled around our journey to see all 30 MLB ballparks. Jenifer and I wanted to take the kids for a week to Washington, D.C. With the September 2014 release of the MLB schedule, we selected a week in early August 2015 when we could see both the Baltimore Orioles and the Washington Nationals play while we were visiting D.C.

The opening of Camden Yards in 1992 changed the way I thought of baseball stadiums. The incredible look of the ballpark and the short outfield walls, where leaping catches robbed hitters of home runs, became some of my favorite teenage memories from watching *Baseball Tonight.*

Many other parks built in the past two decades have tried to duplicate Camden Yards, but the viewing experience, the warehouse enclosed in the park, and the incredible atmosphere make this one of most unique parks we visited, and one of our favorite. I had seen the warehouse from my dorm room in 1995, while watching Cal Ripken Jr. hit a home run the night he broke Lou Gehrig's record. The warehouse existed before the ballpark was built and was such an authentic piece of Baltimore history that the park was built around it. The stadium capacity is over 45,000, but it feels much more intimate when you are actually there.

Most of the seats in the stadium are dark green, but two were replaced with orange ones to commemorate special occasions. The first orange seat marks where Cal Ripken Jr.'s record-breaking home run landed on July 15, 1993, catapulting him into the number one spot on the list of most career home runs by a shortstop. The other orange seat marks the landing spot of Hall of Famer Eddie Murray's 500th career homer, which happened on September 6, 1996. Astonishingly, that home run of Murray's occurred exactly one year after Cal Ripken broke Lou Gehrig's consecutive-games streak. Nearly a quarter of a century after it opened, I thought it was important for Andrew to recognize that Camden Yards completely changed the notion of the modern sports facility.

Andrew and I ate dinner at Boog's Barbecue behind the outfield and watched the first inning of the game from there. We walked around the entire stadium, which was sold out on that Saturday night, and ultimately sat on the third-base side, where the sightlines for watching the game were as good as any stadium we visited. Actually, the stadium provides an incredible viewing experience regardless of where you sit.

The game that night was outstanding. Baltimore was making a playoff push, and the crowd was into every pitch. In his Baltimore debut, Gerardo Parra went one for three and scored a run. Obtained the day before in a trade with Milwaukee, the outfielder became the 1,000[th] player to appear in a game for the Orioles' franchise; he received a standing ovation from many in the sellout crowd of 45,968 before his first at-bat. Manny Machado hit his 23rd home run, to help power the Orioles to a 6–2 victory over the Detroit Tigers.

This game in Baltimore was the first stadium I attended with a *teenage* son. On our trip to Baltimore, Andrew spent a great deal of time on his iPhone, with a little grumpiness that is pretty typical for a 13-year-old. He was getting ready for eighth grade, and we were talking about classes he thought would be tough, stuff his friends were doing in the summer, and what his basketball team might look like. I always enjoy our conversations on road trips, and I shared with Andrew something that concerns me about the college students I work with as a professor. Many of the students I see don't take time to reflect. This is not entirely their fault; young people today, including Andrew, have so much more content, technology, and distractions available to them than I had a generation ago. I don't think this fact is nearly as bad as some parents make it out to be, but I *am* concerned that the constant "noise" distracts young people from looking back at their actions and decisions and examining them critically.

I told Andrew about a student I had in class the previous year who had failed his first exam and came to my office, apologizing for his performance and assuring me he would do better. When he failed the second exam, he returned to my office, apologizing again. When I asked him what he did differently for the second exam, his honest answer was, "Nothing." My hope for Andrew and the great college students I get to teach is that they "own" their mistakes, as this young man did, but also that they take time to reflect on how they can improve. It is all too easy to forget a mistake and get lost in countless Snapchat exchanges or Instagram posts. I have tried hard since Andrew became a teenager to ask him questions that get him to think—not to punish or to relive a mistake, but to help him reflect on how he can have a better outcome the next time.

I was very reflective on this trip to D.C., seeing the Library of Congress, the Supreme Court, and Ford's Theatre all for the first time. I also reflected on the fact that we had reached the two-thirds mark of our goal by visiting our 20th stadium. I told Andrew I thought a lot about the decision he and I had made together six years earlier to try to see all 30 MLB stadiums before he graduated from high school. After the thousands of miles we had traveled at that time and the money spent on tickets, I could honestly tell him how thankful I was we decided to do this. As I reflected on what we had seen and experienced together, I knew there was no journey that I could ever have that would mean more to me as a father.

Fun Facts
Oriole Park at Camden Yards (Baltimore, Maryland)
    1. Seattle Mariners' outfielder Ken Griffey Jr. became the first,

and so far the only, person to hit the Camden Yards warehouse, when he accomplished the feat during the 1993 Home Run Derby.

2. Oriole Park at Camden Yards became host to the first game in MLB history to be played in front of no fans, when the Orioles hosted the Chicago White Sox on April 29, 2015, due to safety concerns from local riots.

3. When Babe Ruth was young, his father owned a building that was a saloon on the bottom level and the family's home on the second floor. That building was known to be located somewhere out in what is now center field at Camden Yards.

21 Nationals Park (Washington)

Love Our Country

August 4, 2015 – National vs. Arizona Diamondbacks

After leaving Baltimore, we spent five full days touring Washington, D.C., as a family. We had an incredible time, and if I could suggest only one city for parents to visit with teenagers, it would be Washington, D.C. It is surprisingly affordable; we visited the Smithsonian's National Museum of American History and National Air and Space Museum, the Supreme Court, and the U.S. Capitol, all for virtually no cost. Our visits to the Lincoln, Jefferson, World War II, and Vietnam memorials were each more moving and poignant than I could have imagined. The Ford's Theatre program, led by a National Park Ranger, was powerful.

Our trip to the Library of Congress produced one of my favorite stories (which I had not heard before the trip). In 1814 when the British burned the Capitol and the 3,000-volume Library of Congress, Thomas Jefferson offered to sell his personal library to Congress as a replacement for the collection destroyed by the British. The former president had acquired the largest personal collection of books in the United States, and Congress purchased Jefferson's library for $23,950 in 1815. The 6,000 volumes he provided helped the Library of Congress survive and supported our young nation. Although many of Jefferson's original volumes were lost in an 1851 fire, through a generous private grant, the Library of Congress now is attempting to preserve the remaining volumes and reassemble Jefferson's library as it was sold to Congress. I loved this story, and Andrew commented that this happened after the things he had studied in school about Jefferson—writing the Declaration of Independence (1776) and serving as the third president of the United States (1801–1809). Despite his advancing age (age 71) and having no official government title, Jefferson was still doing his part to make sure the country was stronger for future generations. I loved the lesson for my children. Whether 13 or 39 or 95 years old, we all have a responsibility to preserve and protect the country that has given us so much.

Our trip to the White House was a little more light-hearted. While we were at the White House Visitor Center, I was looking at an exhibit when I heard the song "Freddy My Love" from the *Grease* soundtrack playing nearby. I commented to Andrew that it was strange someone would be playing music while at the White House, and I continued to hear it for another minute. I was just about to assume that I was being stalked by a *Grease* fan, when Sarah asked if she could play on my iPhone. As I pulled it out of my pocket, I was horrified to discover that it was *my* phone that had been playing "Freddy My Love" throughout the White House Visitor Center! Sarah had downloaded the entire album to my phone after she and I had seen *Grease the Musical* together. I was proudly wearing an Arkansas State University polo shirt that day, and I worried that the other visitors would think people from Arkansas are really into *Grease* or that this 39-year-old man played his own background music no matter where he went. Despite that momentary embarrassment, I have never taken a family trip that I enjoyed more or learned more from than our week in Washington, D.C.

Andrew and I took a taxi to see a Washington Nationals game one night. Nationals Park, opened in 2008 and with a seating capacity of over 41,000, is located in Southeast Washington, south of the Capitol, along the fast-developing Capitol Riverfront adjacent to the Navy Yard. The park features one of the most distinctive plants for which Washington is known: cherry trees. Fourteen Kwanzan

Japanese cherry trees are located in the Center Field Plaza and left-field concourse. We ate before the game in a nice outfield dining section, and the stadium was very easy to walk around while still seeing the action on the field. The Nationals teamed up with the Library of Congress to have a terrific Baseball Americana exhibit located in the concourse area behind home plate. Few stadiums have embraced changing seat colors for historic home runs more than Nationals Park. Blue seats mark where Ryan Zimmerman's walk-off homer landed to win the very first regular-season game at the stadium and the location of Bryce Harper's third-level home run in the 2014 playoffs. These landmarks are fun to see in person and helped us understand more about the history of the franchise.

The game that night featured one of baseball's best starting pitchers, Max Scherzer, who recorded his 1,500[th] career strikeout in the fifth inning but got a no decision. With one out in the bottom of the eighth, Wilson Ramos blooped a two-run single to right field that helped Washington to a 5-4 victory over the Arizona Diamondbacks, and newly acquired Jonathan Papelbon got the save.

The GEICO Presidents Race, in the middle of the fourth inning, is a great highlight at any Nationals' game. Runners dressed as various giant presidents race around the outfield. The lineup of regular racing presidents includes "George" (Washington), "Tom" (Jefferson), "Abe" (Lincoln), and "Teddy" (Roosevelt); other presidents, such as Taft, have had shorter racing careers. Before the game, Andrew and I took a picture with a giant president whom I did not recognize but who had the shortest line for photos. When we got back to the hotel after the game, I looked more closely at the picture and realized it was President Calvin Coolidge. While Coolidge is rarely thought of as one of the greatest or most memorable presidents, he was the subject of an old television commercial my dad would talk about. The commercial was so bad that I would tease him any time he brought it up, and I wondered to myself what marketers at that time could possibly have been thinking. However, going to the game just a few months after my dad's death and taking that picture of Andrew and me, not with Teddy Roosevelt or George Washington, but with Calvin Coolidge, let me know that Dad was still with us on the journey and no doubt smiling as I relayed the Coolidge television commercial to his grandson. Giant president "Cal" raced for only that single season, 2015.

Touring numerous historic locations throughout Washington, D.C., prompted me to tell Andrew that he had won the lottery when he was born. He laughingly asked, "What?" and looked at me with a grin that indicated he thought that my ego must have run away from me. I told him he won the same lottery that I had won, that Jenifer and Sarah had won, and that most of his friends had won: being born in the United States of America. America's distinctive character flows from the wisdom of the Founding Fathers, and the blessings of our freedom play an important role at every stage of life. America—like Andrew, me, and all of its citizens—is not perfect but is, to me, the best place in the history of the world to live.

Baseball, often called "America's pastime," reflects our distinct national character and an unmatched way of life. One of the things we saw everywhere on our journey was the extraordinary ability of baseball to bring together people from every corner of our country who might have nothing else in common. Baseball reflects the best of the American character: It celebrates both teamwork and individual accomplishment, honors tradition and lore, and is uniquely meritocratic, offering people from anywhere the chance to succeed with hard work, dedication, and maybe a little luck along the way.

Fun Facts

Nationals Park (Washington, D.C.)
1. The new Nationals Park became the first major stadium in the United Stated accredited as a Leadership in Energy and Environmental Design (LEED) structure.
2. Pope Benedict XVI celebrated Mass at Nationals Park on April 17, 2008, making it one of the few American sports stadiums to host the Pope.
3. Inspiration for the overall look of the concrete, steel, and glass structure of the stadium was taken from the East Wing of the National Gallery of Art.

22 Petco Park (San Diego)

You Are Not a Self-Made Man

September 6, 2015 –Padres vs. Los Angeles Dodgers

Men's Week 2015 was a little later in the year than usual because an Arkansas State football game over Labor Day weekend provided a chance for us to make a trip to Petco Park in San Diego. I used my Delta frequent-flyer miles to get free tickets to Los Angeles to watch the Red Wolves open the season at USC on Saturday night. We then rented a car the next morning and drove down to San Diego, to see a Padres game before flying home on Monday. The drive down the Pacific Coast Highway from Los Angeles to San Diego provided some of the most magnificent views we have seen anywhere in the country. Plus, we checked off a restaurant we wanted to try when we ate at our first In-N-Out Burger on the scenic drive south.

Petco Park, opened in 2004, is a unique facility that blends perfectly into downtown San Diego. With a seating capacity of over 42,000, it combines modern niceties with some old-fashioned flair. The Western Metal Supply Co. building, once the site of a booming San Diego business that housed everything from car parts to sporting goods, provides historic character and serves as the left-field foul pole. Original plans for Petco Park involved demolishing the building, but it had been given historic landmark status in 1978, which prevented its destruction. Instead, architects helped bring it up to code and included it in the stadium design. What were once storage sheds and offices are now suites, a bar, and a Padres' team store. An example of adaptive reuse, the old building now helps create a unique baseball experience for fans.

One of the most unique features of the stadium is located outside the outfield wall but inside the park gates: The Park at the Park offers fans a nearly three-acre park for enjoyment during games. It contains a mini Little League infield diamond, trees, a statue of "Mr. Padre" Tony Gwynn, and lots of space to sprawl for picnics and play. The stadium has all blue seats that are close to the field and angled toward the pitcher's mound for great sightlines. Petco has a uniquely Southern California appearance, with a white steel and sandstone facade and palm trees placed along the outside. The most memorable scene at the Padres game was the military men and women (over 75,000 military personnel are stationed in San Diego County), in uniform, who occupied an entire section. It was a great opportunity to remind Andrew that no part of our MLB journey would have been possible without the incredible bravery of the men and women who serve in the United States Armed Forces, protecting our country.

The 5–1 Dodgers' victory was a good game, whose outcome was determined by a sloppy play. With the bases loaded in the seventh inning, Padres' reliever Nick Vincent had a two-out, three-base throwing error after fielding Andre Ethier's dribbler up the first-base line. Vincent tossed the ball over first baseman Wil Myers' head, directly in front of where Andrew and I were sitting, allowing three runs to score. Carl Crawford, who was a former Ray and one of Andrew's all-time favorite players, stole one of the last bases of his career, and Justin Turner scored two runs to help the Dodgers win.

On our drive to San Diego for the game, shortly after enjoying our meal at In-N-Out Burger, Andrew and I were listening to a podcast in which the interviewee referred to himself as a "self-made" man. I think I startled Andrew when I paused the program to ask him never to use that phrase. It's one of the phrases I most dislike. As a father, I want my children always to appreciate the fact that others made the rode they travel and the opportunities they have possible. I am a first-generation college student, and I was able to go to college due to the financial sacrifices of my mom who worked for a staffing service and my dad who was a mailman. I had professors who invested in me, and I had co-workers, like Tom Payne, early in my career who saw something in me and helped me to develop my confidence and professional talents. I am proud to say that I am *not* a self-made man, and I am thankful for the people who have helped me at every stage of my life.

On the way back to Los Angeles, Andrew and I were hungry and stopped at a Costco to eat dinner. My 13-year-old son was in his eating prime, and we decided we would each get three items. When our number was called, the employee handed us two slices of pizza, chicken tenders, a barbecue sandwich, a hamburger, and a hot dog. It was so much food that I looked around me: Did the employee combine our order with that of a woman and children standing nearby, who might be mistaken for part of our family and eating some of this huge order? He clearly did not; when we went to the counter, he slid three trays of food to us and smiled as he said, "Enjoy your glorious feast." We did, and Andrew and I still laugh about this today.

As we were finishing our meal after a great day, our discussion turned to the military men and women we had seen in uniform at the Padres game. I repeated to Andrew that he is not a self-made man, and beyond his family and friends, I wanted to him to understand that those young people, not much older than he, are volunteering to serve in the military. Their sacrifice allows us the freedom and security to have days like the one we had just had.

Fun Facts

Petco Park (San Diego, California)
1. Instead of having the batter face east/northeast like many other stadiums, Petco Park was built specifically to have the batter face north, to highlight the beautiful San Diego skyline as well as the Bay.
2. In 2014 Petco Park became the only open-air baseball stadium in the United States to host a Davis Cup tennis match. The contest between the United States and Great

Britain was played on a temporary red-clay court in left center field that was constructed at a cost of $750,000.

3. The largest attendance ever at a college baseball game was at Petco Park when the new stadium hosted an NCAA-record 40,106 fans for a game between San Diego State and the University of Houston on March 11, 2004.

23 Comerica Park (Detroit)

Our Best Days Are Ahead of Us

September 25, 2015 – Tigers vs. Minnesota Twins

In January 2015, my dad attended his last college football game, when Arkansas State lost the GoDaddy Bowl game to the University of Toledo, a team that was already on our schedule to play nine months later. Andrew and I decided to drive to Toledo, Ohio, for the rematch in late September, when we hoped the Red Wolves would bounce back with a win. We also would make the fairly short drive from Toledo to Detroit, to see the Tigers play at Comerica Park the night before.

Comerica Park, which opened in 2000, is filled with terrific details that add to the game atmosphere: the stone tigers that encompass the park, the home-plate–shaped dirt track around the field, and the retired numbers and names above the outfield wall. Comerica has a seating capacity of over 41,000, and the stadium fits perfectly into the new downtown atmosphere in Detroit. Another impressive feature was the Comerica Carousel, an ornate carousel featuring 30 hand-painted tigers and two chariots, which is located at the base of the food court behind the first-base area. The Tigers celebrate six of their all-time great players with a series of statues located along the left-center field wall. They are cast in stainless steel and feature some of the greatest Tigers in history: Ty Cobb, Charlie Gehringer, Hank Greenberg, Willie Horton, Al Kaline, and Hal Newhouser. Each is perched atop a granite pedestal and reaches about 13 feet in height. We also really liked a unique in-game feature that occurs when any of the Tigers' players hits a home run: The eyes of the two tigers standing on the top of the scoreboard light up, and the sound of a growling tiger can be heard throughout the stadium.

Our seats on the first-base line offered an amazing view of downtown Detroit on a fall evening. Detroit was out of the pennant race, but Minnesota was competing for the last wild-card spot in the American League. Rajai Davis hit a two-run home run off Minnesota's Glen Perkins in the eighth inning, and the Tigers rallied for a 6–4 victory over the Twins. Neftali Feliz, a young, hard-throwing closer whom we had seen in our visit to Texas in 2010, pitched the ninth inning and recorded the save.

One of the things I hope Andrew takes from our ballpark journey is to never lose his optimism. As much as anything, I hope he always believes that our best days are ahead of us. In the years leading up to our trip to Comerica Park, Andrew and I had often discussed the economic challenges facing the city of Detroit. He was old enough to remember the GM and Chrysler bankruptcies and the numerous media stories about how Detroit had fallen from a major industrial city to a place where life was tough for its residents. While Andrew and I waited in a line to get Little Caesars Pizza (the Tigers were owned at that time by the man who owned Little Caesars), 13-year-old Andrew kept saying how impressed he was by the stadium. When I asked him what he liked best, he answered that it was so much nicer than what he thought it would be, based on all that he had heard about Detroit.

The people we met at the game and visited with shared a similar optimism. While a great downtown ballpark does not fix all of the challenges Detroit or other cities face, I hope Andrew remembers the optimism we saw in Detroit when he faces challenging times. I want him to remember that even in the face of personal and professional challenges, he has the ability to overcome them. I want him, as an old man whose body does not work the way it once did, still to have an optimistic belief that his best days are ahead of him. I have seen too many people of all ages complain that they wish they could go back to another time, or they wish they were younger, or a host of other negative arguments about the present and the future. Such feelings do nothing but take away the opportunity that today brings to love, laugh, and make a positive impact on the world.

While it is easy to be optimistic when everything is going your way, it is tougher to be so when you face challenges. It was inspiring to see the optimism in Detroit, a city that had gone from being a finalist to host the 1968 Summer Olympics to a city characterized by economic struggle and population drain. I think the experience helped encourage Andrew to be optimistic, even when things are not going well. If he does poorly on a math test, gets dumped by a girl he likes, or doesn't get every promotion he seeks in his career, I know that keeping his optimism can help him with any challenge in his life.

In 2017 I watched the incredible 18-hour Ken Burns documentary about the Vietnam War and was moved by the powerful reflections of the people who fought in it. During the two weeks I was watching it, I read a fascinating article by Dr. Dennis Charney, the dean of the Icahn School of Medicine at Mount Sinai, that touched on the benefits of optimism. Dr. Charney had examined approximately 750 Vietnam War veterans who were held as prisoners of war for six to eight years. Tortured and kept in solitary confinement, these 750 men were remarkably resilient. Unlike many other veterans, they did not develop depression or post-traumatic stress disorder after their release, even though they had endured extreme stress. After extensive interviews and tests, Charney found 10 characteristics that set them apart, and the top one was optimism. Even in the most horrific of circumstances, those POWs found optimism, and it helped them to survive.

If those brave veterans and the city of Detroit can be optimistic with all they have been through, there is absolutely no reason Andrew, or I, or any of us should let challenges in our daily lives strip away the optimistic belief that great things are ahead.

Fun Facts

Comerica Park (Detroit, Michigan)
1. One of the most unique features of Comerica Park is the stripe that runs from the pitcher's mound to home plate. It is

often referred to as the "keyhole," due to the look of the stripe combined with the pitcher's mound.

2. Comerica Park has no seat with an obstructed view.
3. Comerica Park has its very own Ferris wheel, with each car shaped to look like a baseball.

24 Citi Field (New York)

Be More Grateful than Proud

August 10, 2016 – Mets vs. Arizona Diamondbacks

We took our first family vacation to New York City in the summer of 2016, and once again we planned the dates so that we could see two teams, the Yankees and the Mets, while we were there. The plan was to see two Broadway shows (*The Phantom of the Opera* and *The Lion King*) and then two baseball games. Jenifer, Sarah, and my mom wanted to shop one of the nights we went to see baseball, leaving Andrew and me to take a taxi to the Mets' game on a Wednesday night. The taxi ride out to Queens was pretty rough. There was no air conditioning in the cab, and the starts and stops through New York traffic made me think Andrew's first action upon entering Citi Field might be to throw up.

Andrew powered through, and we were very impressed by the stadium when we arrived. Everything at Citi Field, which opened in 2009 and seats just under 42,000, feels first-class. As a fan of baseball history, I was impressed with how Citi Field manages to honor the two previous homes of the Mets, Shea Stadium and the Polo Grounds, while also paying tribute to another historic New York stadium, Ebbets Field. The grand rotunda at the entrance to Citi

Field is a dead ringer for the famous marble rotunda at Ebbets Field in Brooklyn. Founded in 1962 as one of baseball's first expansion teams, the Mets are big on their history. The Mets Hall of Fame & Museum, located adjacent to the Jackie Robinson Rotunda on the first-base side of the stadium, features artifacts and interactive kiosks that focus on special Mets' moments, plus highlight videos celebrating the Mets' biggest feats.

One of the most unique features inside the stadium is the seats that extend over the field of play. These overhangs are low enough and jut out far enough that deep fly balls to right field can lead to plays that continue under the seats of fans, who can't see what's going on. Andrew and I discussed that those overhanging seats must make for some interesting nights for Mets' outfielders throughout the season. The Citi Field Fan Fest, located on the concourse behind center field, provides everyone the chance to take a picture with two of baseball's most recognizable mascots, Mr. and Mrs. Met. The food selection at Citi Field is probably the best of any MLB stadium we visited. One of the highlights of this game for Andrew and me was our first trip to the packed, but outstanding, Shake Shack restaurant in the outfield concourse.

The ageless Bartolo Colón, who was at the height of his social media fame, started the game, and the Mets' Kelly Johnson forced extra innings with a two-run homer in the ninth off Arizona closer Jake Barrett. Ultimately, Oscar Hernández hit his first major league homer in the 12th inning, leading the Diamondbacks to a 3–2 win over the Mets that night.

Early in the game, a guy ran up to us after seeing our Arkansas State University shirts and said he knew the school's former basketball coach, John Brady. He asked if we would take a selfie with him, the only such request from a total stranger we had on the journey, and he tweeted out the picture. I smiled and told Andrew afterward that there clearly are Red Wolves groupies anywhere you go.

One of the biggest things I have stressed to Andrew over the years is to say "thank you." I am certain he has tired of me asking him if he said thank you, probably more so since he has been a teenager. One time, he told me that he had already said thank you and didn't want to look stupid by saying thank you again, to which I replied that I have yet to see someone get upset about being thanked twice. Beyond saying thank you, I want my son to have an attitude of being grateful. The culture that 14-year-olds live in encourages them to be proud about everything they do, to post their highlights and accomplishments on social media so the world will know. In trips to Times Square, the NBA store, the Empire State Building, and throughout our trip to New York City, I saw Andrew posting more than usual. We are all guilty, every now and then, of wanting to impress those around us. But at some point, we have to ask ourselves, what purpose does this behavior actually serve?

Gratitude is an emotion that relates to our ability to feel and express thankfulness and appreciation. Researcher Robert Emmons has been examining gratitude through a psychological lens for many years and has found that expressing gratitude improves mental, physical, and relational well-being. The research findings also suggest that being grateful affects one's overall experience of happiness, and these effects tend to be long-lasting.

I was not part of Emmons' research project, but I can assure Andrew that I have experienced this same impact on my life from being grateful. I do not know what tools, distractions, and technology will be available when Andrew starts a family or is my age, but I am confident that seeking to be more grateful than proud will benefit every aspect of his life. I told him on the trip that I bet he will make sure his children say thank you often, just as I encourage him to do. After all, being grateful is one of the few things in life that is timeless.

Fun Facts
Citi Field (Queens, New York)
1. When a Mets' player homers, a 16-foot-tall, 4,800-pound apple, decorated with a Mets' logo that lights up, emerges from the center field, hitter's background at Citi Field. The idea of the apple is a holdover from Shea Stadium. An alcove at Citi Field was created to house the modern apple, which rises 15 feet in about three seconds.
2. Citi Field is the only ballpark in the major leagues to sport non-yellow foul poles.
3. As a marketer, I love that the LED Coca-Cola sign, found above the Coca-Cola Corner behind right field, changes colors. It is usually lit up red for the brand, but it changes

colors for special occasions. For example, a red, white, and blue flag waves through the lettering during the singing of the National Anthem; sometimes the sign will light up with the Batman logo when Mets' pitcher Matt Harvey, nicknamed the Dark Knight of Gotham, comes on the field.

25 Yankee Stadium (New York)

Prioritize Love

August 12, 2016 – Yankees vs. Tampa Bay Rays

After a busy, hot day visiting the Statue of Liberty, our family took the subway all the way to Yankee Stadium. Walking up to the new Yankee stadium, which opened in 2009, we were impressed with the size of the facility and the classic design touches.

The new Yankee stadium has many parts that are similar to the old one, including the outside walls of the stadium, color of seats, size of the playing field, and bullpen placements. Cavernous concourses give way to open spaces, with sightlines to the field from nearly every vantage point in the stadium. With a seating capacity just under 50,000, Yankee Stadium is the largest ballpark in the American League. A 56-foot by 101-foot high-definition video scoreboard is located in the outfield. One of the most famous parts of the stadium is Monument Park, which is located beyond the outfield fence in center field, below a restaurant that makes up the "batters eye" (the background in the outfield that the hitter sees when at bat). This open-air museum consists of plaques, monuments, and retired numbers honoring renowned New York Yankees.

When I bought our tickets for the Yankees' game against the

Tampa Bay Rays during our family trip in 2016, nobody could have known that it would be the last game for one of the best players in the history of baseball. If you ask for my personal rankings, the five best players I have watched in my life are Barry Bonds, Mike Trout, Pedro Martínez, Ken Griffey Jr., and Alex Rodriguez. The weird set of circumstances that led to this being Rodriguez's last game made it probably the most unusual game of any stadium we visited. Jenifer, Sarah, and my mom all joined us for this game, even though StubHub prices for our tickets skyrocketed after the A-Rod announcement. The highlight of the game itself came late: At the start of the ninth inning, with the sellout crowd of 46,459 chanting "We want A-Rod!," Yankees' manager Joe Girardi sent Rodriguez to third base for the first time in 15 months, as the organist played "Thanks for Memory." It was indeed a memorable moment.

In the game, Starlin Castro had four RBIs for the Yankees, hitting a tiebreaking, two-run homer in the sixth off Chris Archer (one of Andrew's favorite pitchers) that gave CC Sabathia the win. A-Rod did not have a chance to make a defensive play in the ninth inning because Dellin Betances struck out all three Rays' hitters to finish out the 6–3 Yankees' victory. A-Rod played well but did not homer in the game, finishing his career with 696 home runs, fourth on the career list at the time behind Barry Bonds (762), Hank Aaron (755), and Babe Ruth (714).

Alex Rodriguez has been one of the most famous athletes for most of my adult life, someone recognized around the world. Andrew mentioned something about how famous A-Rod was, leading to a good discussion about my fear, as a father, of young people wanting to be famous for fame's sake. A study I read said that high school students today would choose being the personal assistant for a celebrity such as A-Rod over being the president of Harvard University. Being "famous" has become an increasingly popular goal for young people. As we discussed fame, I asked Andrew, "How does that end up? What do you do when you stop being A-Rod's personal assistant? What happens when you are no longer famous?" This is a great challenge for our society, in which fame can be achieved through many avenues, many of them self-destructive, and often leaves young people unable to live happily outside the limelight.

When the time ran out on A-Rod's career, what was next? There was a great lesson for Andrew and for me that night. As A-Rod left the stage, the people who were with him—his daughters and his mom—were the people who were his life. Fans would turn the page to new players; co-workers and friends move on or have different priorities throughout their lives. Your family is who is there when you walk off the field. The people you love and who love you define who you are.

Too many of us (we can all fall victim to this from time to time) use social media to create a caricature of our lives, in which only the highlights are displayed. We have all seen movies whose best parts were shown in the previews, and we are left paying our $10 or more to watch two hours of boring or bad storytelling. There are two major problems with immersing ourselves in these social media caricatures: The first is that we then compare our normal lives (and whether you are A-Rod, you, or me, we all have normal lives) to other people's highlights shows. Such comparison may encourage people to feel sad or jealous or upset that they are not living a similar "great" life.

The other problem is that once we post our own daily narrative, what do we do with the other 23 hours of the day? Even if other people see only the good parts we posted, we see *all* of our own lives—all of the faults, missteps, heartbreaks, successes, and failures. When our taxi got back to our hotel, we watched *SportsCenter* for about 30 minutes, and Andrew was surprised that there was not more coverage of A-Rod's last game. When the game was over that night, just like at a movie, the people got up at the end of the game and left. People had moved on to thinking about NFL training camps, other pennant races, and their own lives. But A-Rod's mom, his daughters, and the people who loved him would always be there.

Before we went to sleep that night, I repeated for Andrew that it is important always to prioritize love. I love baseball, and I love Arkansas State University, and I love watching *King of Queens* reruns, but what I love *most* is Andrew and Sarah and Jenifer and my mom and dad Their love for me, and my love for them, defines who I am and who they are. Prioritizing love is essential to successfully navigating through our lives.

Fun Facts

Yankee Stadium (The Bronx, New York)

1. At a cost of approximately $1.3 billion, Yankee Stadium is the most expensive stadium ever built in Major League Baseball.
2. The Yankee Stadium grounds crew performs the "YMCA" in the middle of the fifth inning during every game.
3. After every home game, the Yankees play Frank Sinatra's recording "New York, New York."

26 Citizens Bank Park (Philadelphia)

Just Because You Are Good at Something Doesn't

Mean It Is What You Are Meant to Do

August 13, 2016 – Phillies vs. Colorado Rockies

We had driven to New York City and decided to drive back home through Philadelphia, in order to see a Phillies' game. Philadelphia is a city that has really grown on me over the years, and we spent the afternoon before the game walking around Independence Mall. This incredible square mile is filled with history, from the Liberty Bell to Independence Hall to the National Constitution Center. I highly recommend it to any family visiting Philadelphia.

Citizens Bank Park, which opened in 2004, is located four miles from downtown, in the South Philadelphia Sports Complex, which has four stadiums and arenas standing next door to each other. Only a sea of parking spaces in the Sports Complex separates Citizens Bank Park from Lincoln Financial Field (home of the Eagles), the Wells Fargo Center (home of the 76ers and Flyers), and Xfinity Live! (a dining and entertainment complex). The Sports Complex is similar in feel to the Royals' Kauffman Stadium and its shared space with Arrowhead Stadium and the Kansas City Chiefs of the NFL. The stadium capacity is 43,651, and at least some of the playing field is visible no matter where you are in the ballpark. The downtown skyline is visible from much of the upper deck, and the view on that clear August night was outstanding.

The lower deck at Citizens Bank Park features a very pleasant concourse (that we walked) which wraps around the entire ballpark. In the outfield, the concourse turns into Ashburn Alley named in honor of Phillies' legend Richie Ashburn. Ashburn Alley is home to many of Citizens Bank Park's best food options: Geno's Steaks serves up world-famous Philly cheesesteaks, and Chickie's & Pete's offers signature Crab Fries. From one-way glass inside the Diamond Club, you can view the Phillies' indoor batting cage; it is carpeted with the turf from the Phillies' previous home at Veterans Stadium and lined with that stadium's original outfield wall. We loved seeing one of the best mascots in all of baseball, the Phillie Phanatic, perform throughout the game. The fun-loving ambassador of Phillies' baseball can be spotted all around the ballpark. In the game we saw, he performed on the field at the end of the fifth inning and on the Phillies' dugout in the bottom of the seventh inning.

The game between the Phillies and the Colorado Rockies featured two teams who were really struggling at the time. It was homecoming weekend for the Phillies, and many of their legendary players, including Mike Schmidt, Steve Carlton, and a retiring Randy Wolf, were introduced before the game. Maikel Franco, who was on my fantasy baseball team that year, hit a three-run homer, then later was in the middle of a testy exchange that led to the benches clearing and a pair of ejections. The Phillies beat Colorado 6–3 on that hot, humid Saturday evening, with a game time temperature of 93 degrees and a heat index of 105. The other Phillies' player on my fantasy team in 2016, Jeanmar Gómez, pitched a scoreless ninth, stranding two runners, for his 30th save in 33 opportunities. Andrew and I celebrated at the end of the game with a handshake and hug because we had now seen every National League stadium.

The Phillies' game was at the end of a great week with our family in New York City. I loved this time together, and as Andrew and I sat at the game, I thought how little I was excited about returning to the office on Monday. I had been dean a little over two years at this point and was still one of the youngest business school deans in the United States, but I missed being a professor. I missed teaching more students, I missed writing, and I missed the flexibility to do the things I felt were most important. I shared with Andrew that I thought I was ready to resign as dean at the end of the current academic year, and he immediately asked, "Why would you do that?"

This was a difficult conversation for me as a father. I was very proud of what the College of Business had done during my time as dean, and I had the great privilege to work with incredible faculty, staff, and students. In that moment, the best thing I could think to say was a quote I had heard years before: "Just because you are good at something doesn't mean it is what you are meant to do." This quote is handy for lots of discussions with children. I have seen numerous kids over the years spending much of their free time doing something they are good at, but don't really enjoy. The value of time (discussed earlier in the book) was not something I appreciated as a teenager, but as an adult, I know more: Andrew has a precious number of days to be a kid, and I have a precious few days to be his dad while he is still living at home.

One of my favorite parts of being dean was the weekly Friday tours I would give to prospective Arkansas State University students and their parents. At the end of the tour, I would summarize why I thought this was a great place to choose for college and would always say, "I am more of a professor than I am a dean, and more of a father than I am anything." Sitting in Citizens Bank Park and talking with my son, I knew I was ready to spend more time being a professor and more time being just dad.

I think Andrew appreciates the time we have been blessed to spend together, and I hope he remembers this lesson across all aspects of his life. What his mom or I, his friends, classmates, co-workers, and others want pales in comparison to what he knows in his heart he is meant to do.

Fun Facts

Citizens Bank Park (Philadelphia, Pennsylvania)
1. We went to more stadiums in August (12) than in any other month during our ballpark journey.
2. The NHL paid $900,000 for a new, Bermuda grass field in Citizens Bank Park after the Winter Classic contest featuring

the Philadelphia Flyers ruined the old field. It's the furthest north the sturdy grass has been tried in a stadium.

3. A gigantic replica of the Liberty Bell (50 feet high and 35 feet wide), accompanied by a Citizens Bank Park sign, is located in right center field above the rooftop bleacher seats. Towering 100 feet above street level, the Bell lights up and "rings" after every Phillies' home run and victory.

—

27 Target Field (Minneapolis)

Seek the Grace of Humility

May 26, 2017 – Twins vs. Tampa Bay Rays

After our trip to Philadelphia, I told my wife that I would try to finish our journey in 2017. We had tentatively planned a family trip to Minneapolis for Memorial Day weekend if the Twins were in town. When the 2017 schedule came out, we were thrilled to find that the Tampa Bay Rays were making their only trip to Minnesota that weekend.

We arrived on Friday, dropped Jenifer and Sarah off at the Mall of America, and headed for our 27th stadium. Target Field is a nice ballpark in a very nice city. The park, opened in 2010 with a seating capacity of just under 40,000, still felt very new. Target Field is the only Major League Baseball stadium built on top of a railroad line. The tracks pass underneath the grandstand on the third-base side, and the oval-shaped structure in the northeast corner is the entrance for railroad passengers. The light rail system for urban commuters passes behind the bleachers and scoreboard beyond left field, and a large parking garage looms beyond right center field. Andrew commented that the scoreboard looked huge; the 57-foot-tall, 107-foot-wide scoreboard is one of the five largest in all of Major League

Baseball. We both liked the limestone backstop and wall next to the left-field foul pole and the overhanging upper decks in the outfield that make the stadium feel intimate. The upper deck is partially protected by a large canopy, with heated concourses, restrooms, and concessions, to help fans deal with cold weather during the season. My favorite touch at the stadium was the great Twins' logo high above center field, showing Mr. Minneapolis and Mr. Saint Paul shaking hands across the Mississippi River.

Minnesota also wins the prize for the nicest usher at any stadium we visited. Our seats were in the first row in right field, and our usher was an older gentleman who had worked games for a number of years. He walked over and told us how glad he was that we were at the game. He said how much he likes the new ballpark and how much better it is than the Metrodome, where the Twins previously played. We told him about our ballpark journey and that this was our 27th MLB stadium. He came back later with a program and a Twins pen, because, he said, he wanted Target Field to stand out in our memory. His kindness and positive spirit definitely do stand out in our memories of that day.

The Rays won the game behind a dominating pitching performance by Chris Archer and home runs by three of Andrew's favorite players: Kevin Kiermaier, Logan Morrison, and Steve Souza Jr. Souza also provided one of the most memorable plays of our entire journey: he dove for a line drive when the ball was close to 30 feet from him. It happened right in front of us, and the fans (and Souza's teammate Kevin Kiermaier) joked about the play for the rest of the night. Center fielder Kiermaier doubled over laughing while watching the replay. When Souza stepped to the plate in the eighth inning, the Twins showed the replay of the dive on the video board, and the crowd gave a tongue-in-cheek standing ovation. A good sport, Souza smiled as he stepped into the box, then belted his eighth homer into the second deck in left field, as part of the Rays 5–2 victory.

This was the first game on the ballpark journey when Andrew was taller than I was. He was now a little over 6 foot 2 inches and in great shape, and his junior high basketball team had won the first district championship in their school's history. He did very well academically as a freshman in high school but would sometimes respond sarcastically to me when I mentioned something he already knew. Success and good fortune can cause all of us to get a little full of ourselves as we get older, and I encouraged him on this trip to find the grace of humility. Andrew had heard me, many times, give him my marketing-professor advice that a person, a brand, or a non-profit needs to promote itself to communicate value. As a marketer, I will always believe that, but one thing fatherhood helps teach you is the liberating power of humility. Although the tendency to self-congratulation is no new phenomenon in our society, the outlets for it have increased enormously, with numerous social media platforms providing young people with the ability (and often pressure) to impress others.

David Brooks wrote in his book *The Road to Character*, "Humility is the awareness that there's a lot you don't know and that a lot of what you think you know is distorted or wrong." I love that quote and have often told new fathers that you could substitute the word "humility" with "being a dad." As Andrew gets older, he will continue to get smarter and have more information at his fingertips than people in my generation could imagine, but he should not mistake that he in fact knows everything or has life completely figured out. I shared with him that humility provides you the peace to know that there will always be people richer and poorer than you are, people who are smarter and better looking, people who have overcome obstacles that you will never face. Emotional strength is not about ego or being right or wrong; it is about showing love and grace in a world filled with flawed human beings.

As for the sarcastic responses to information and advice he is given, I urged Andrew to try always to receive correction graciously, seek constructive feedback, and be quick to forgive. There is so much we all can learn and improve upon, if we just listen to people who care about us. Andrew and I talked about mistakes he had made or something he said that hurt someone's feelings, and then discussed how humility allows him to grant himself the same forgiveness he asks of others. Andrew shares my love of history and one of my favorite historical moments is the humility shown at the end of the Civil War. After that horrible war and all of the bloodshed, Lincoln and Grant and Lee had the humility not to brag or curse or punish, but to serve each other and the nation in order to try to heal our broken Union.

The grace of humility has helped me be a better father, and I hope it will help Andrew to move forward from setbacks, overcome challenging times, and find peace that will enhance every part his personal and professional life.

Fun Facts

Target Field (Minneapolis, Minnesota)

1. Target Field's footprint is only 8.5 acres large—the smallest in Major League Baseball.
2. Target Field is the first baseball-only park for the Twins. Prior to Target Field, the Twins had shared the same sports venue with the Minnesota Vikings (Metropolitan Stadium and then the Metrodome).
3. Target Field's facade is built with more than 100,000 square feet of limestone mined from southwest Minnesota.

28 Rogers Centre (Toronto)

Don't Think Like a Computer

June 18, 2017 – Blue Jays vs. Chicago White Sox

For most of the first 27 stadiums we visited, we had a personal or professional reason to be in that city during baseball season. When we got to the final three ballparks, I told Andrew we would make special trips to see each one so that we could finish in 2017. First up was a Father's Day weekend trip, when Jenifer, Andrew, and I drove from Andrew's summer-league basketball game in Pocahontas, Arkansas, to Toronto and back in four days. Toronto is a great city, and we enjoyed shopping and seeing a movie the night before Andrew and I attended a game at Rogers Centre.

An architectural marvel, Rogers Centre is home to Major League Baseball's only Canadian franchise. Rogers Centre is a massive stadium in downtown Toronto with a seating capacity of over 48,000. When I was a kid, I would see pictures of the stadium—then named the SkyDome. To me, it seemed an iconic space-age stadium, with cameras in the bullpen, television monitors in the dugout, and a retractable domed roof. There even was a hotel inside the stadium that overlooked the outfield. The Rogers Centre Renaissance Hotel is still part of the stadium; 70 of its 350 rooms overlook the playing field. During the game Andrew and I saw a majority of those rooms actively watching the action, and I regretted that I did not think to stay there as part of our trip.

On this Sunday afternoon, the roof was closed, preventing a great view of the massive CN Tower which had impressed us as we wandered around Toronto earlier in the trip. We read about Rogers Centre's roof system, which features one stationary panel and three moveable panels. Panels 2 and 3 slide on parallel rails, while panel 1 slides on a circular rail "tucking" underneath 2 and 3. Although the stadium, originally opened in 1989, has aged well, its design often feels very '80s; for example, its numerous thin hallways rarely have views of the field, in contrast to the large open concourses at many newer parks.

Despite both teams having losing records at the time, the Toronto fans impressed Andrew and me with their passion for each at-bat. There was a great Father's Day crowd of 46,599 to watch the Blue Jays defeat the White Sox 7–3 behind home runs by Russell Martin and Kendrys Morales. Troy Tulowitzki had two hits for the Blue Jays, and I remembered watching him play in 2006 when he was a young prospect for the Double-A Tulsa Drillers. I had picked up free Minor League tickets at a local QuikTrip convenience store, and it was a fun break, with four-year-old Andrew, from the stress of completing my Ph.D. that summer.

When we had started our ballpark journey in 2008, no one in our family had any type of social media profile. That was very different as we made our way to Toronto in June 2017: Andrew spent much of the trip Snapchatting and Instagramming with his friends. Teenagers today sometimes get a bad rap for wanting to spend so much time on social media; the truth is, I think, that most of us would have done the same thing if it had been available when we were that age. I remember my dad getting frustrated with me because I would stay up too late in the summer using the new three-way-calling feature on the phone in my room. Technology will continue to change, but 15-year-olds will always find ways to interact with their friends.

Andrew was happy when he found out we had an international bandwidth plan on his phone, so he did not have to go an entire weekend unconnected. I, however, was a little sad about this. As technology advances, I often hear people worry about advances in artificial intelligence and the danger of computers thinking like humans. I told Andrew on this trip that, as a father, I am more worried about him thinking like a computer. He looked perplexed as we discussed this idea, but I wanted him to understand that the analytics that drive computer decisions are not always the best choices for people. Computers don't see the humanity in situations; they don't display empathy or make ethical judgments. Andrew argued that you can find the answer to almost any question using a smartphone; my argument back was that you can't always find the *right* answer. Computers are great at finding facts, such as who won the NBA championship in 1984 or the highest-grossing movie of all time. But they struggle with good answers about how to treat people or how you can find peace, joy, and contentment in your life. Their algorithms don't really teach you how to love the people who mean the most to you.

Our culture has made it harder to do good, to work on things that don't generate a return on investment or a positive metric on the spreadsheet of our time. Thinking like a computer probably means you never give money to charity, never say I am sorry, never do something for someone that they can't repay. I remember a friend sending me an email when Andrew was born about how much it costs to raise a child to age 18 (the current estimate is over $233,000) and what other investments could be made with that money. I have no computer program or spreadsheet to prove it to you, but being a dad has been the best investment of my entire life. The love I have for Andrew and Sarah and the experiences we have had together cannot be easily summarized by any computer program.

Computational thinking can likely improve the efficiencies in Andrew's daily life. It can't, though, give him empathy that enables him to put himself in the position of the person he is interacting with. And most importantly, thinking like a computer can't provide him the relationships or the experiences that make life worth living.

Fun Facts

Rogers Centre (Toronto, Ontario, Canada)
1. The game in Toronto was the only game we attended on Father's Day.
2. Opening in 1989, the SkyDome, now Rogers Centre, was the

first stadium with a retractable roof, allowing any sport to be played indoors or outdoors, year-round.

3. The Blue Jays became the first team to attract over four million fans in one season (1991).

29 Fenway Park (Boston)

Keep Your Eyes on the Road

July 28, 2017 – Red Sox vs. Kansas City Royals

Even though I had been to several Major League Baseball stadiums before Andrew and I started our journey, I pledged to him that I would not finish seeing all 30 before he did. Since I had been to Fenway Park and I knew we would be finishing in Oakland a couple of weeks later, we flew from Memphis to Providence, Rhode Island (which offered a lower fare than Boston).

This was one of the most relaxing trips on our ballpark journey. I had left my role as dean a month earlier and was thrilled to return to the faculty and be named the R.M. "Bob" Wood Endowed Professor in Sales Leadership and Professor of Marketing. The endowed professorship meant a great deal to me. I can remember telling my parents on our first trip to see the Arizona Diamondbacks that one of my professional goals was to have an endowed position before I was 50 years old—a goal I achieved. The second edition of our marketing textbook had been published in the summer and was doing well, and I felt a great sense of personal and professional contentment. Andrew and I rented a car, and thanks to the navigational tools in my iPhone, we drove from Providence right to

Fenway in about an hour.

Fenway is a true classic stadium and an American landmark. The oldest park in Major League Baseball has become the toughest ticket to get (seating capacity is under 38,000) and is a bucket-list item for many baseball fans. One of the most impressive things about Fenway Park is how the Red Sox organization has kept the park's nostalgic look and feel while updating so much of the inside to provide a great experience for fans. Yawkey Way, a short street outside the stadium, resembled a neighborhood street party, with music, food, souvenirs, juggling, and more. Andrew and I both felt a family-type atmosphere that I can't remember feeling at any other stadium on our journey.

Once inside, Andrew and I were both hungry and knew exactly what we wanted to eat first. The Fenway Frank is the most unique hot dog we ate on our ballpark journey. The meat is delicious, and the buns are New England hot dog rolls, which are long, leavened, unsweetened rolls with flat, white, crustless sides. We walked over and saw the red seat (Section 42, Row 37, Seat 21) where on June 9, 1946, Ted Williams hit a mammoth blast to right field, 502 feet from home plate.

The atmosphere at Fenway for the entire nine innings was incredible, and the fans were passionate throughout the game in a way that I have rarely seen at any sporting event. We had great outfield seats (bought on StubHub), and my seat was right next to the Green Monster, Fenway's famed left-field wall. It is the highest outfield wall in baseball but is located only 310 to 315 feet from home plate. The Green Monster wasn't really born until 1947, when advertisements were scraped off the wall and painted green to match the rest of Fenway. In 1975 the wall was covered in hard plastic, giving it the motif it has now. I remember being impressed as a marketer when Red Sox ownership wised up to the allure of the Monster and installed 269 seats atop the Green Monster in 2003. Those seats are consistently some of the toughest tickets to get at any baseball stadium, and they were full on that Friday night.

There was lots of anticipation for the game because David Price, who had a very public argument going at the time with Red Sox Hall of Fame commentator Dennis Eckersley, was scheduled to start. Andrew and I had watched Price get his first Major League win during our visit to Tampa Bay eight years earlier, and we suggested to each other that he would be wise to learn the lesson we had discussed in Cleveland (see Chapter 8) and say, "I'm sorry." By the time we arrived at the game, it was announced that Price had suffered an injury, was back on the disabled list, and would be replaced by Rick Porcello as the starter. Salvador Pérez and Mike Moustakas homered as the Royals extended their winning streak to a season-high nine games with a 4–2 win over the Red Sox, to the delight of an entire Kansas City fan section in the top deck of the stadium.

Andrew spent some time studying on our trip to Boston. It was summer, so he was not looking over English or math but was reviewing the rules he needed to know for his Arkansas driver's test. He would not take Driver's Ed until the school year, but he first needed to pass the written exam to obtain his learner's permit. At 16 years old, I was certain I was a great driver. (They would not have given me a license otherwise, right?) But looking back on it now, I was terrible, and I wanted Andrew to know that. It was purely by the grace of God that I survived those early driving years; as Andrew's father, it scares me to think about how inexperienced I was when I first started driving.

Teaching Andrew to drive an automatic transmission seemed far easier than what my dad had to go through: I pounded the clutch and would bolt out from stop signs, scaring us both. Andrew had picked up his high school schedule a couple of days before we left for Boston, and probably the class we talked about the most on the trip was Driver's Ed. He seemed less than impressed with my stories of my driver's ed experience—driving a Chevy Lumina with our high school wrestling coach and practicing on the driving simulator that had been built in a mobile-home–looking building on the high school campus. The main thing I remember our driver's ed teacher saying over and over was simply, "Keep your eyes on the road." For the next several days and on the plane to Boston, I would see Andrew studying the driver's book, and I would in the background say, "Keep your eyes on the road."

My teenage self thought the instructor's comments were simple advice, given in the hope that I wouldn't wreck the Lumina and hurt all of us in the car. As a parent, the advice now meant something different to me. I made the statement to Andrew again at the game, and he seemed annoyed by it, as teenage children can sometimes be, but I wanted him to understand what I meant by it. For kids Andrew's age, receiving a driver's license is a rite of passage that marks a whole new level of independence and freedom. It is mobility come of age and represents the opportunity to handle greater responsibility. For parents, particularly when children start to drive or when they begin college, we need to understand that our kids must be given the privacy and independence required to become adults. I know this is true, even though it feels like I have lost much of the control that I think I have had all of his life. I want Andrew to keep his eyes on the road so he can see the opportunities ahead *and* also the pitfalls that come along the way.

Many new drivers keep their eyes straight ahead even when they're turning the car, and I want Andrew to remember to look where he wants the car to go. More importantly, I want him to always be looking where he wants his life to go. I asked Andrew what he wanted his life to look like in 10 years. I asked him to think about what he wanted his education, career, and relationships to be at that time. It was fun to hear his answers. I could tell he had thought a great deal about some things and hardly at all about others. I wanted him to know that all of those things and more are possible as long he stays focused on the journey ahead. In the weeks after we finished the ballpark journey, and we got closer to Andrew's 16th birthday, I kept telling him to keep his eyes on the road, and I hope he always appreciates what I am really telling him.

Fun Facts

Fenway Park (Boston, Massachusetts)
1. Fenway Park is the oldest park in Major League Baseball, having opened on April 20th, 1912.
2. The Green Monster is 37 feet and a pair of inches high, built first out of wood, then concrete and tin, and now hard plastic. It stretches 231 feet across Fenway Park's left field, with three of those feet in foul territory.
3. The Neil Diamond song "Sweet Caroline" has been played in the middle of the eighth inning at every game since 2002.

30 Oakland-Alameda County Coliseum (Oakland)

Know What Really Matters

August 8, 2017 – Athletics vs. Seattle Mariners

On a cool Tuesday night in August 2017, Andrew and I got on board a free Holiday Inn shuttle that took us to see our 30th Major League Baseball stadium. Attending a game at the Oakland-Alameda County Coliseum is a little like stepping back in time. Long before Camden Yards started the modern baseball-ballpark movement, I grew up in the 1980s watching games in multi-purpose stadiums like Three Rivers Stadium, Riverfront Stadium, and Candlestick Park that were home to both MLB and NFL franchises. By the time we got to Oakland on our ballpark journey, Oakland Coliseum was the only stadium left that also housed a full-time NFL team, the Raiders. Despite the announcement earlier that year that the Raiders' franchise would be moving to Las Vegas, there was equal amounts of Athletics' and Raiders' signage and promotion throughout the stadium, which to us was unusual to see.

Since it was the last stadium on our tour, I purchased front-row tickets down the third-base line. Despite row one being printed on our tickets, we were not as close to the action as some games we had attended, because no stadium in baseball has more foul territory than the Oakland Coliseum. I have read that statisticians believe that the large amount of foul territory takes 5 to 10 points off every hitter's batting average in Oakland. Consistent with its multi-purpose use, Oakland Coliseum has variable seating, depending on the sport: 47,170 for baseball (eighth largest) and 56,057 for football (second smallest). Over a decade before we visited, the A's closed all sections of the upper deck at the Oakland Coliseum, moving fans closer to the action on the field and attempting to make the stadium feel more intimate. The stadium, which originally opened in 1966, was easy to get to, and attending on a Tuesday night meant there was free parking for the game. (The only other stadium where we saw free parking offered was Tampa Bay.)

The game itself was entertaining. The A's got off to a fast start, led by a first-inning home run by Khris Davis (who was on my fantasy team that year). Seattle battled back, and Leonys Martín homered in the top of the 10th inning, as the Mariners rallied from a four-run deficit. The game ended when Edwin Díaz got rookie Matt Chapman, who was not old enough to drive when we started our ballpark journey, to fly out, for Díaz's 24th save of the season and a 7–6 defeat of the Athletics that night.

After nine years and thousands of miles, I sat at the game amazed that we had seen every MLB stadium together. When we finished our ballpark journey, I was asked by numerous people what I remembered most about our trip. It is difficult to pick one story, one funny moment, or one great play over others. I started the trip with a 6-year-old little boy and finished nine years to the day later with an incredible 15-year-old son who is taller than I am.

While it is hard to choose what I most fondly remember, I do hope that as Andrew gets older and becomes a dad himself, he remembers these three things forever:

First, I love him with all my heart. One thing that happened at every ballpark is that I told Andrew that I love him. Andrew has heard me say it (maybe more times than a teenage boy prefers), and I want him to know every second of his life how proud and blessed I am to be his dad. I have often said in speeches or recruiting events that being a marketing professor at Arkansas State University is the best job in the world because of the students I get to teach and the incredible people with whom I get to work. The truth is the job of professor is the *second-best* job in the world. The *best* job in the whole world is being a dad.

Our ballpark journey has been one of the great adventures of my life. I love Major League Baseball, and I love the unique things about each stadium, but most of all I love that Andrew and I did it together. The memories of this trip will be with us forever. They bring me joy every time I turn on a baseball game and see a place we have been.

Second, the journey was fun because we did it together. Our modern world provides so many great opportunities and technologies that were pure science fiction when I was Andrew's age. Despite all the amazing tools at our fingertips, the most important moments in my life still involve spending time with the people I love. It took us nine years to finish the journey; the little boy I took to the first (Arizona) game started Valley View High School the following Monday. I also loved the great family and friends with whom we saw games during the journey, including Jenifer and Sarah, my mom and dad, my father-in-law, Philip Tew, Patricia Robertson, Nelson Taylor, Tim Padgett, Andrew Todd, Cortney Kieffer and her family, and Steve Hudson.

The ballpark journey that Andrew and I shared also inspired Sarah and me to launch our own father-daughter adventure: to see all 59 national parks before she graduates from high school. (We had seen 20 when Andrew and I finished the ballpark journey in Oakland; we have a little more time to complete this goal, as she started fifth grade the next week.) I am thankful that my wife, daughter, and mom have been enthusiastic supporters of the ballpark journey, and I know my dad (who went to 10 stadiums with us before he passed away) is smiling down from heaven, proud that we finished this great journey.

Third, we completed our goal and finished our journey! Nine years earlier, on my parents' wedding anniversary, I took six-year-old Andrew away from watching *Phineas and Ferb* on the television at the hotel to his first MLB game. We decided that day to set an ambitious goal of seeing all 30 MLB stadiums together by the time he graduated from high school, and we finished it. I never wanted to be a dad who started lots of things but never finished them, and I don't want Andrew to be that type of father, husband, or professional either.

David Brooks' outstanding book *The Road to Character* talks about the difference between "résumé" virtues and "eulogy" virtues, and the book had a profound impact on how I think about fatherhood. As I finish this book, statistics say that I have about 40 years left to live. While I am going to plan financially that it will be more than 40 years, the deaths of my dad and José Fernández serve as a constant reminder that I might not have even 10 more minutes. Regardless of whether it is one day or 60 years from now, I am quite confident that most people at my funeral won't really care about the books I have written, where I got my academic degrees, or how I invested my money. I am, however, very confident that this journey with my son will be something that Andrew and others will remember and share.

We set this goal and completed this journey together. Baseball is America's pastime—an incredible sport and a multi-billion-dollar industry—but what I think of during any game I now see on television is: (1) I have been to that stadium, and (2) I loved getting to be there with my son.

As I was sitting at the Oakland Coliseum watching the A's versus Mariners game that final night, I was full of joy, excited for the start of a new school year for both of us, thankful that we had the opportunity to share this adventure together, and blessed to have such an outstanding son, whom I love with all my heart. We will go to new stadiums as they are built in the years ahead, and I told Andrew that if any of his children want to see all 30 stadiums one day, I have plenty of Red Wolf polo shirts to make the roundtrip ballpark journey all over again, with them.

Fun Facts

Oakland-Alameda County Coliseum (Oakland, California)

1. The A's were the only professional tenant of the stadium from 1981–1995 while the Raiders played in Los Angeles.
2. There is an underground tunnel that connects the A's stadium to Oracle Arena, the home of the Golden State Warriors. This tunnel became famous during the 2016 NBA Finals when Warriors' star Draymond Green, who was suspended for a game, was at the A's game, planning to use the tunnel to get back to Oracle to celebrate another World Championship. That did not happen, however, as LeBron

James and the Cleveland Cavaliers won that game and ultimately that series, four games to three.

3. In 2017, the Athletics dedicated the Coliseum's playing surface as Rickey Henderson Field in honor of MLB Hall of Famer and former Athletic Rickey Henderson.

AFTERWORD

by Andrew Hunt

OK, wow, did I think I would ever help write a book? The answer is a huge and ginormous *no*. I have never thought of myself as a big book guy, though I have had to read plenty over the years. I've been part of my high school's accelerated reader's program, in which each book is worth a certain number of points and there are goals for the number of points you need to get. The most memorable of the books I've read were Colt McCoy's *Growing Up Colt* and Tony Dungy's *Quiet Strength*. I was inspired by the life stories in those books. I strive to be an athlete like Colt McCoy and to act around others like Tony Dungy. So I hope that even one of you reading this book can feel the same about my dad or me and will appreciate and recommend this book, like I do McCoy's and Dungy's.

Now to the good stuff: I have so many great stories from this trip and am eager to share some. Let me start by saying that when the Tampa Bay Rays win the World Series, I want to be on that field celebrating with them. As my dad discusses in the book, I am honestly the biggest Tampa Bay Rays' fan on the planet earth. Every year, I have an ongoing lunch wager with Sam, a friend who plays on our high school basketball team with me, about the Rays making the playoffs. Unfortunately, I will probably have to buy Sam lunch at the Rodeo, one of our favorite restaurants in Jonesboro, because I don't see the Rays making it to the playoffs this year (but I'll keep the faith). I have tried to win other fans for the Rays; my friend Olivia is now probably the second-biggest fan of the Tampa Rays, at least in the state of Arkansas.

When people hear about our baseball journey to all 30 MLB parks, someone usually asks what my favorite park was. Even as a huge Rays' fan, my favorite is not the Trop. It happens to be Miller Park, the home of the Milwaukee Brewers. When we first pulled up to that venue in 2010, it blew me away. Keep in mind this is before I ever went to a WrestleMania or to any venue of that size. I believe my exact words were, "Daddy, this is soooooooooo GINORMOUS." Not only was the park amazing, but the crowd was very involved the whole game. So, yeah, it obviously holds a special place in my heart. Also, the very first *Intentional Talk* (my favorite baseball show) I ever watched took place there, with Brewers' announcer Bob Euecker talking to "my guys" Chris Rose and Kevin Millar (the show's hosts). Maybe after this book gets released, you-all could get me on an episode, please and thanks.

My next-favorite story is about the 2015 World Series between the Kansas City Royals and the New York Mets. My dad and I had talked for ages about going to a World Series, and Kansas City is one of the closest Major League cities to our home. We discussed going to Game 1 of the Series; however there was chance of bad weather, and we didn't think it was worth missing a couple days of school just to go to a rain delay. So the next day in eighth grade, with my horrible-looking buzzcut, I was distraught and couldn't focus. (By the way, thanks to my friend John Maurras, for his advice to grow out the hair.) That night around 8 or 9 o'clock I thought about Game 2. Now the reason I had a tough choice to make about going was that my favorite basketball team, the Memphis Grizzlies, was playing LeBron James and the Cleveland Cavaliers in their NBA season opener. I'm not going to lie: I was very stressed about this decision. It might sound crazy, but I just didn't want to look back later and think what a bad decision I had made. Ultimately, I chose the World Series because *it's the World Series!* Most parents would've been, like, "Nope, it's way too late." However, my dad's reaction was, "OK, great." He went to StubHub, bought and printed those tickets, and we left our house around 10 o'clock. (Game 1 was still going on.) Amazingly, we were on our way to Kauffman Stadium to watch Game 2 of the 2015 World Series.

The atmosphere at the game was awesome; the only event I can even compare it to is maybe a WrestleMania or a Memphis Grizzlies' playoff game. I knew I made the right decision as soon as we got to the stadium because we saw one of the most iconic people in sports today, Marlins Man. If you don't know who that is, he is the person in the front row of all the major sporting events wearing all Marlins' clothes. I got to witness not only a great atmosphere but also a great game. Johnny Cueto shut down the Mets as the Royals managed to get a few runs on Jacob deGrom, which I didn't think was even possible. As soon as that game was over, I knew 1,000 percent that I had made the right choice. However, I am glad that my parents put me in that situation. Looking back on it, the experience gave me a really good lesson on decision making. I decided to choose what would last a lifetime rather than a few days. The experiences and memories that last a lifetime will help when life throws you a curveball. Plus, when I saw the Grizzlies lost by 30 to the Cavs that night, my decision looked even better.

In his retirement speech, Lou Gehrig famously said, "I consider myself to be the luckiest man on the face of the earth." I'm not so sure he was at that time, but I can assure you that I feel the same way. Maybe it's just baseball that makes you feel that way. You always hear about how wonderful it is when you see a father and son playing catch in the backyard. Not only did I get to do that, but I got to travel with my dad and see America's favorite pastime played in all 30 Major League Baseball parks. There is not one thing I would trade that experience for, and I am so glad I got to do it with the best dad there is. I wasn't confined to a space my whole childhood and told to study. I got to travel all over the country, learning lessons that are priceless, things you could never find in a textbook (even my dad's). Now whenever I see a televised baseball game, I have so many great memories to look back on as I watch. I have done everything as a baseball fan that I've ever wanted to do, and I am barely 16. Well, everything except watch the Rays win the World Series, with me there at the game.

Anyway, I hope that the story of our baseball journey can inspire a parent to create for his or her child as many memories and stories as I have. I don't necessarily remember what happened last week at my house; I might've been playing a little NBA 2K or MLB® The Show™. However, I can remember vividly what happened 10 years ago at Chase Field. Give your kid something to remember other than just school. As the Northwestern Mutual commercial says, "Spend your life living." So after you finish this book, go start, now.

The collection of baseballs in Andrew's room that we bought at each park we visited in order starting with Arizona and then finishing with Oakland.

ABOUT THE AUTHOR

Dr. Shane Hunt grew up in Oklahoma City, Oklahoma. After completing his undergraduate and MBA degrees at the University of Oklahoma, Shane went to work for a Fortune 500 company in Tulsa and spent eight years working as a pricing analyst, product manager, and business development manager, overseeing numerous mergers and acquisitions initiatives. Shane received his Ph.D. in Marketing from Oklahoma State University, where he was an AMA Sheth Foundation and National Conference in Sales Management Doctoral Fellow.

Shane is the recipient of the 2010 National Inspire Integrity Award from the National Society of Collegiate Scholars and the 2010 Lt. Col. Barney Smith Award as Professor of the Year at Arkansas State University. Shane's research has appeared in *The Journal of Personal Selling and Sales Management* and *The Journal of Business Logistics,* and he has been invited to present to numerous organizations including the American Marketing Association and the National Conference in Sales Management. Shane serves as the R.M. "Bob" Wood Endowed Professor in Sales Leadership and Professor of Marketing at Arkansas State University.

Shane lives in Jonesboro, Arkansas, with his wife, Jenifer, and their two children, Andrew and Sarah.

Made in the USA
Coppell, TX
26 December 2019